Charles Trombley, formerly an enthusiastic Jehovah's Witness, was very sure that miracles didn't happen anymore. Miracles were okay for the apostles and the infant Church, but those days were over.

But finally the time came when he became the father of a baby girl with club feet, and he found himself desperately *needing* a miracle. . . .

Things began to happen when Trombley decided to bypass theory and pray for a miracle anyhow. The man who really wanted to know the truth found not only the miracle of that beautifully answered prayer but the miracle of a victorious life knowing Jesus Christ.

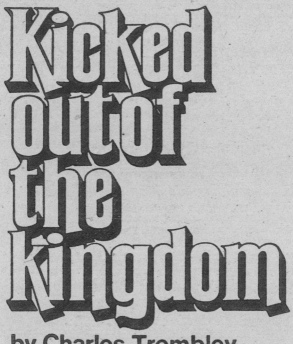

Kicked out of the Kingdom

by Charles Trombley

Whitaker House

504 LAUREL DRIVE, MONROEVILLE, PA 15146

Kicked Out of the Kingdom
by Charles Trombley

Copyright © 1974
by

Whitaker House
504 Laurel Drive
Monroeville, Pennsylvania
15146

ISBN 0-88368-044-0

Printed in the United States of America

Dedicated to Gladys, David, Darlene, Debbie and Deanna, who were all involved in this miracle-story.

CONTENTS

FOREWORD

The book of the Acts of the Apostles in our New Testament should be called the book of the Acts of the Holy Spirit. And the book doesn't really end, it just quits.

The Holy Spirit has never stopped performing His miracles. Although for centuries their number was both greatly diminished and largely ignored by the church, that is no longer the case. Today, fresh and powerful winds of revival are sweeping through the musty halls of denominational Christianity. Dramatic manifestations of God's miracle-working power once more abound in the lives of those who love Jesus Christ, even as they did in the first century. We are living in the days the prophets promised; those days when God is pouring out His Spirit "on all flesh."

The book you are about to read is a classic example of that outpouring. It is also a classic example of how faith can revolutionize human life. It is the dramatic account of how God's power wrenched a husband and wife free from the prison of a dead religious cult through the healing of their infant daughter and then plunged them into the living reality of New Testament Christianity.

I know Charles Trombley personally. I have

shared the same ministerial platform with him. I have observed his ministry across the years and thank God for the lasting fruit of it.

As you read this book you will share the faith, the joys, the frustrations, the fears and the victories, but most of all the sheer spiritual excitement which is the heritage and which should be the experience of every believer in Jesus Christ.

Another exciting chapter has been added to the unfinished book of Acts.

—Don W. Basham, author of
Face Up with a Miracle

PREFACE

Many other signs therefore Jesus also performed in the presence of the disciples, which are not written in this book; but these have been written that you may believe that Jesus is the Christ, the Son of God; and that believing you may have life in His name.

The Apostle John*

In a court of law, only personal evidence is acceptable. Anything less is rejected as hearsay and factually unreliable. *"That which we have seen and heard declare we unto you,"* was the basis for John's testimony; therefore it is admissable as acceptable evidence. The purpose of this testimony is to provide, from a former Jehovah's Witness, a personal account which, added to all the other evidence, proves that the age of miracles is not over—and that we serve an unchanging Christ.

Christians frequently strive to defend their particular doctrines with raw, cold theology, keeping themselves personally uninvolved. It is not my purpose to defend any system of religious thought, but to declare simply and honestly what Jesus has done in our lives. I say "our lives" because this testimony personally involves two people: my wife and myself.

* John 20:30, 31, New American Standard Bible.

11

Since childhood, I'd been a bit rebellious about the "normative" status of the church. When I read or heard about the thrilling adventures of Jesus and the early believers, something in me cried, "Is *my* church for real, God?" Sitting passively in a pew, singing unenthusiastic songs, and listening to a droning sermon left me questioning.

"Take it by faith, son," my elders said. "We had to!"

"Don't even talk like that, Chuck. God'll getcha!"

Still I cried the louder, "Where are You, God? Come out, wherever You are! If You're alive and if You're actually present, *please* make Yourself known!"

He finally answered that cry in a most unusual way. This book is the account of a series of miracles which led me to the answer. A number of fictitious names have been used in order to protect confidences.

Charles C. Trombley

CHAPTER ONE

"YOUR DAUGHTER IS CRIPPLED!"

I still remember the expectancy I felt as I watched the white uniformed nurse help Glad into a wheel chair and hurry her toward the delivery room. She had deliberately waited until the last minute, and we barely got to the hospital in time.

"Mr. Trombley? Let's fill out these insurance forms and get them out of the way," the admitting clerk suggested.

She pointed to a chair beside her desk, indicating I should be seated while she typed in the necessary information: name, address, telephone, employment, etc. Then she directed me to the fathers' waiting room. Picking up a dog-eared copy of *Life* magazine, I skimmed through it, but didn't remember anything I read.

"Why doesn't someone invent something that will fill this kind of vacuum?" I thought.

"What're you doing *here?*" a familiar voice inquired after a few minutes. It was Dr. Tatum, our family physician, peering over the top of his thick glasses.

The unexpected sound of his deep voice startled me. I jumped from the chair and met him head-on in the doorway.

"Here?" I jested. "I *live* here, remember? I've

13

only been here a few minutes—twenty to be exact. What're *you* doin' *here?* Has anything happened yet? Is Glad all right?"

"Why, didn't you know?" he answered with a mischievous grin. "You have a daughter!"

"Already! Wow! That was quick. When can I see them?"

"In a few minutes. Let's sit down over here!" Taking me by the arm he gently led me to two side-by-side chairs. "After the nurses finish up you can see her."

Looking at me, he paused for a moment as though choosing his words carefully. Suddenly I felt an overwhelming sense of uneasiness.

"There's something I have to tell you," he began. "I'm not an expert on birth defects, so I suggest you have a specialist check the baby's feet."

The humor was drained from his long, narrow face which had been so cheerful a moment before.

"For what?" I demanded impatiently. "What's wrong?"

"Her feet don't look normal. Dr. Lee is a bone specialist who visits the clinic here every two weeks. He's from Deaconess Hospital in Boston, and he's quite good—" He paused again, drawing in a deep breath. "Make an appointment—just to be sure!"

My heart was pounding. Turning in my chair, I looked deeply into his eyes.

"Just what do *you* think is wrong?" I demanded.

"They look like clubfeet," he replied. "Both feet turn in suspiciously. There isn't anything I can do for her, but Dr. Lee specializes in bone deformities." He rose, started to leave, and then

14

turned toward me. "Why don't you go see your wife now?"

Without saying anything more, he walked briskly toward the doctors' lounge.

Bewildered, I sat there for a few minutes, thinking that less than half an hour before, Glad and I had walked into the hospital filled with anticipation and hope. Since we already had a son (David was two), both of us wanted a daughter; but with clubfeet? A cripple? A cold, foreboding fear gripped me. I knew Dr. Tatum expected me to tell Glad, but I didn't have the courage then. I'd wait until tomorrow; she had been through enough for one evening.

Two nurses and one male attendant were pushing Glad's stretcher out of the delivery room when I saw her. She looked radiantly happy, although her eyes were tired. Darlene (the baby's name had already been chosen) was beside her, snuggled in her right arm. With mingled excitement and dread, I followed them to the room. After the nurses left, Glad turned to me.

"Chuck," she said, her voice still groggy from the anesthetic, "her face has a funny blue color, but the nurse said she'd be all right. I'm concerned about her feet, though. They don't look good. When I asked the nurse about them, she shushed me and told me to be quiet. Why would she give me a brush-off like that unless something's wrong?"

There wasn't enough moral strength in me to tell her then. Deftly I changed the subject and talked about other things. After a while I left, telling her I'd see her in the morning.

15

The next day Glad wanted to talk about the baby's feet again. "Chuck, I just have the awfulest feeling that something's really wrong," she said fearfully.

"Why, what do you mean?" I replied.

"Oh, I don't know—the nurse acts worried. When she brought the baby in this morning, her face seemed drawn."

"Maybe she had a fight with her husband," I kidded, trying to dismiss the matter lightly. I doubt if she heard me.

After a long moment's silence, Glad asked the question I'd been dreading: "Chuck, did the doctor say anything about the baby's feet?"

"Well, nothing much," I said, beating around the bush. "He did mention that there might be a small problem. . . ."

"What kind of problem?"

"Well, he wasn't quite sure."

"But what did he say?"

"Glad, I hate to tell you this." I put my arm around her. "He said it might be clubfeet."

She didn't say anything. But I felt her shoulders trembling, and saw the tears running down her cheeks. I was completely lost for words.

During the following two weeks, Glad and I suffered together as we considered the outcome. "Can the bone doctor really help her, or is Dr. Tatum just stringing us along?" we asked each other. "What if he can't do anything? What then? Will she ever walk normally?"

By the time Dr. Lee visited our small hospital in Bellows Falls, Vermont, we had mentally accepted the baby's deformity as fact; but we were both

16

upset and were wondering what we had done to deserve such a misfortune.

After his preliminary examination, Dr. Lee confirmed Dr. Tatum's suspicion. "Your daughter has clubfeet!" he informed us without any hint of evasion.

"What does this mean, and what can be done for her?" I asked.

"Well . . ." he began slowly, "it means that without proper care she'll be crippled for life; but we're able to help most of the cases today. First, we'll put plaster booties on her feet and legs. When she's older and stronger, we can have some shoes fitted with special braces. And, if necessary" —he paused momentarily to study our reactions— "when she's four or five we can begin some corrective surgery. But we hope we won't have to go that far."

Immediately my mind had visions of mountains of bills, surrounded by deep valleys of heartaches and pain. Why did such a thing have to happen to us?

"She'll wear the casts two weeks at a time," he continued. "Then we'll give her a rest for two weeks before putting on new ones. During the two weeks she's without them, her feet must be massaged twice daily and then wrapped in bandages. We'll do everything we possibly can for her."

When we brought Darlene home that day, each leg was encased in a white plaster cast up to the knee. Those casts anchored Darlene to the bed as effectively as if she were tied there. Consequently she fussed almost constantly, even though Glad changed her position repeatedly.

17

When the casts were removed after two weeks, Glad faithfully and lovingly massaged the little feet twice a day; then carefully bound them in place with flannel bandages. After Darlene's two weeks of freedom were over, new casts were applied and she was again made almost immobile. This cycle was repeated several times, and still the feet looked the same.

One evening I arrived home from work, more tired than usual. Trying to hide my weariness, I bounded into the house.

"Hi, Glady, I'm home!" I expected her to meet me with my usual greeting and kiss, but she wasn't there. From the day we were married, she had always walked me to the door when I left and met me there when I returned. Today, something was wrong.

After waiting a moment, I called again. "Glady, where are you?" Everything was still.

Then I heard soft sobbing in the bedroom. Apprehensively, I walked across the living room and stopped at the doorway to the bedroom. Glad was standing over the bathinette, the baby lying in front of her. Her eyes were red from weeping.

"What's wrong, hon?"

"Look at these feet," she sobbed. "I just brought her back from the clinic and she isn't any better."

Standing by her side, I picked up the tiny feet which had been hidden in plaster booties for the last two weeks. They hung loose and were turning inward to the point that the toes nearly touched the inside of the leg. Tenderly I pushed them to their normal position, but when I released the pressure they hung as limp as though they were broken. Glad was right; they weren't any better.

"What can we do?" I asked helplessly.

"Can't we pray for her? We pray for many other things," she pleaded. "Let's pray that Jehovah will heal her!" Her voice took on a note of urgency, as though some new kind of hope was springing to life.

"All right," I replied, "we'll pray!"

Tenderly we each laid a hand on her, as though directed by some inner instinct. Then holding on to each other like lost children, we prayed: "Jehovah, if it is Your will, and if You can, will You heal our baby?"

It was a simple, childlike plea for help, even though my mind cried out with unanswered questions. After we said "Amen," I slipped quietly out of the bedroom while Glad finished dressing the baby. Dog-tired from the day's work and wearied with a new kind of mental confusion, I slumped into my chair in the living room and tried to think it through.

Why do these situations have to be so complex? Why does our knowledge of God and of the conditions for answered prayer have to be regulated with *do's* and *don'ts*? "Careful, Chuck," I mused, "you're dangerously close to blasphemy."

For several years I had been brainwashed with the teaching that the days of miracles had ceased with the death of the apostles and those on whom they laid their hands. IF a miracle should take place —they *don't*, mind you—but if one *should* take place, then the *devil* did it. This was the kind of indoctrination I had received from the Watchtower Society, which claims to be the sole channel of communication between Jehovah and man and the only authorized interpreter of Bible truth. If I

19

really believed what I had been taught, how had I had the audacity to ask God for a miracle?

As I sat there musing over my problem, I overheard Glad in the bedroom talking baby talk to Darlene. *She* sounded cheerful enough now, but my spirit was as dull and depressed as the snowless winter landscape outside the living room window.

How had I gotten involved with the Witnesses in the first place? I suppose it was the end result of a notable lack of Bible teaching in the denominational church I'd attended as a boy, plus my own indifference to the little I *had* been taught. Mentally and logically I knew God *was*—but He seemed so detached and untouchable. I visited churches of several other denominations, only to conclude that they were as badly off as mine, if not worse. It seemed to me that they were only play-acting. Why were the services always the same? Why was their singing so lifeless? And why did the minister act so spiritless, if he really believed his message?

"God, I know You're there somewhere," my heart cried. "But where? Why are You so hard to find? Are You deliberately hiding? I know *about* You, but I don't *know* You!" But no answer came.

It was something during this period of questioning that I started studying Watchtower helps. Their books were free, easy to read, and contained many scriptures.

Salvation, the Witnesses declared, was *earned* by going door to door, preaching the gospel of the Watchtower, and "maintaining integrity" toward Jehovah and His earthly Organization. If enough "points" were earned, they would tip the scales in your favor when Jehovah judges the world at Armageddon. If you were found "worthy" or "good" enough, then you'd be entitled to enter the New World Society of Jehovah's Witnesses and live on earth as a physical human being for one thousand years. During this time, you'd be on continuous probation, proving to God that you were worthy to eat of the Tree of Life and live forever.

At first their doctrines sounded "way out"—but the more I read, the more I found myself believing them. In the beginning, I read only out of curiosity; but without realizing it, I was allowing my thinking to be systematically altered. Unconsciously, I began using the Witnesses' terminology, mouthing their arguments, and placing my faith in their connection with God rather than in God Himself.

Ultimately I was hooked. I had to settle somewhere; and the Society had the most to offer, it seemed to me. Its members studied their Bibles more than other groups; and who else in Christendom obeyed Jehovah's command to make His name known? After I had made the commitment, some of my inner tension was relieved.

One area of grave doubt remained, however. The heart and core of the Watchtower gospel is that Jesus returned secretly in 1914, when He "raptured" (raised up to heaven) all the "sleeping saints." (Glad's father, Papa Allen, didn't agree with this, though he was an active Witness for years.) Since 1914, the Witnesses said, Jesus has been ruling "in the midst of His enemies" (the churches of Christendom) and directing His Kingdom through the Society.

But if Jesus was actually ruling the earth now, why wasn't He making Himself known? Why hadn't we seen any evidence of His power?

21

To an outsider this might not seem like much of a problem; but to me it was vital and fundamental. If Jesus was real, if He was alive, then why did everyone rely on "proof-text evidence," with each one proving his point with a battle of words? Why didn't anybody know Jesus personally?

The other part of my problem was just as profound and just as unanswerable. The Bible said that neither God nor His Word changes. Yet it appeared that He *had* changed! Throughout the pre-Christian ages, God had made Himself known through His mighty acts: keeping the children of Israel, sustaining them, healing them, and punishing them when necessary. And it had been the same during the earthly ministry of Jesus: The sick were healed, the blind were given sight, and those possessed with devils were delivered. But *now,* according to what I had been taught, God had changed, and there were no more miracles. This puzzled me a great deal. Hadn't Jesus commanded His disciples, and later the whole church, to go and do the same works *He* did?

Of course, the Society comforted me by saying, "God's purpose in making Himself known through miracles was to provide a stop-gap witness for Himself until the Bible was written and the church was mature. Then miracles wouldn't be needed any longer!"

Big deal! Such reasoning bothered me—especially when I thought about Darlene's feet.

Does God heal or doesn't He? Is sickness the will of Jehovah? If Darlene's deformity was His will, then it didn't seem right for us to try to correct it. Should we attempt to free ourselves from God's will by medicine, if He wants us sick?

By this time, Glad was preparing supper. I rose wearily from the chair and walked back into the bedroom to look at the baby again. Noticing that Glad had not wrapped her feet and legs with the bandages, I questioned her about it when I went into the kitchen.

"It just didn't seem right," she explained. "We asked Jehovah to heal her, didn't we? Let's wait!"

CHAPTER TWO

HE DID IT!

Three days later I was playing with the baby in the middle of the living room floor, when something caught my eye. At first I thought I was imagining things. Perhaps my strong desires had burst the bounds of reality and forced me into a world of make-believe—but those feet certainly looked normal! My immediate reaction was to call out for Glad, but I resisted the urge.

"I'd better check and make sure," I said to myself.

I looked at the feet again. The limpness was definitely gone and instead of turning inward, they pointed straight ahead. Taking one of the delicate legs with my right hand, I gripped the foot with my other hand and gently tried to turn it inward. It wouldn't turn!

Almost frightened, I released the foot, expecting it to return to its limp state, but it remained in place. I tried again, and the same thing happened. Excited now but thoroughly bewildered, I dropped that foot and tried the other one, with the same results.

I rose to my feet and stared unbelievingly at those feet a second longer—and then the full impact of what had happened exploded in my mind.

"Gladys, come here—quickly!" I shouted in a tone I reserved for emergencies.

"Wh—wh—what's the matter?" she asked fearfully, seeing the baby on the floor in front of me. "What're you doing?" Pushing past me, she knelt down and picked Darlene up.

"Take a look at those feet! Has something happened to them or am I just imagining things?"

She stared at me blankly and then briefly inspected the feet while my words filtered into her consciousness. Even though we had prayed for the baby's healing we had never witnessed a miracle before and the shock of it left us stunned.

I showed her how I had tried to twist the feet, and again they remained normal.

"See? You can't move them like we could before."

Darlene started to whimper and I realized that in my excitement I was hurting her. Glad's eyes were building little crystal pools of tears as she threw her arms around my neck.

"He did it! He did it! Do you realize . . . this is a miracle?"

If it's possible to laugh for joy and cry for happiness at the same time, that's what we did. Amidst our tears and smiles, we rechecked the feet again and again to reassure ourselves that it was real. It was! Our baby was healed!

"He did it!" I shouted again. "Jehovah healed her! He still heals today!"

Sane, sensible Glad reminded me of my manners. "Yes, He did and we'd better thank Him right now," she urged.

So we stood there, our arms wrapped around each other and the baby between us—and we thanked God the best way we knew how.

"Praise Jehovah! Thank You, Jehovah," we said over and over and over and over. How easily the words flowed! How completely effortless it was to praise Him! I don't remember having ever praised the Lord before; but then, this *was* a rather special occasion!

Supper that night was a happy mixture of spasmodic eating, excited talking, and uninhibited joy. Our religious friends would have said we were "emotional." Later, after Glad had finished the dishes and put Darlene and David to bed, we sat and reminisced about the events that had led up to that day.

"Do you remember when my mother sent us that healing magazine?" Glad asked.

"I couldn't forget it," I replied. "I didn't much agree with it then."

Glad's mother had found a copy of *Dead Men On Furlough*, a book about Communism, and on the back cover was an order blank for a free magazine. Out of curiosity, she sent for it. When *Wings of Healing* arrived, its sixteen pages were filled with messages and testimonies of healings, complete with names and addresses. The whole approach was *so* foreign to the unchangeable format of the *Watchtower* publications that it annoyed me. Perhaps I should say the positiveness of its message left me threatened. After glancing at it, I threw it aside. "It's a devil's lie" was my comment—the typical Watchtower Bible student's explanation of anything he didn't understand. But that magazine had left its mark on my mind.

Glad left the supper table and walked to the large picture window. Looking out across the field to the farm she said, "Do you remember that Sunday afternoon when we went to the farm and found Papa listening to that radio preacher?"

"You mean the one who was praying for the sick? What was that silly thing he asked them to do?"

"What do you mean?" Glad asked.

"Wasn't he the one who told the listeners to put their hands on the radio as a point of contact, and said that Jesus would heal them in their homes?"

I remembered it all right. In fact, it was some time before I could forget the impression that it left. How could somebody pray over the radio and expect God to heal someone miles away? "Anyway," I had convinced myself, "God doesn't heal any more!"

"You know, Glad—the thing that bugged me was that your dad halfway acted as though he *believed* it. He even had tears in his eyes. But what really surprised me was his reply when you asked him what was the matter."

"Me too," Glad replied. "I'll never forget how he looked up at us and said, 'Wouldn't it be wonderful if that could be true?'"

"Actually, I wondered if his age wasn't warping his thinking," I said. "Now I wish he were here so I could apologize. Wouldn't he rejoice with us to see Darlene healed?" (He had died a few weeks before Darlene's healing.)

As Glad and I called to mind the many incidents that had subtly influenced our thinking in recent weeks, I could come to only one conclusion: This was God's doing!

Glad apparently arrived at the same conclusion

at the same time, for she suddenly jumped to her feet and shouted, "Chuck! Can't you see? The Lord has been preparing us all along. Do you realize that we never heard anything about healing before Darlene was born, and since then we've come across it several times? See? Jehovah has been planting the seed, like when Mother gave us that magazine, and—and—then the radio program. And now look at what we've got: a *miracle!*

CHAPTER THREE

THE DAY OF DISCOVERY

"Poor Chuck! He's really flipped this time!" some of my friends said regretfully when they heard that I'd decided to investigate the teachings of divine healing.

"Healing and miracles aren't for today. Doesn't he know that?" others commented.

Keeping my contemplations to myself, I quietly withdrew from all Kingdom Hall activities, including my book studies and field time, knowing that sooner or later someone would be sent to check up on me. In the meantime, I began my search.

From the outset, I knew I couldn't depend on Watchtower study aids, since I already knew what *they* said! Likewise, I refused to consider any outside books or helps. My childhood days in my home church had spelled exactly "nothing equals nothing," and I couldn't chance any more of *that!* Consequently, God forced me to look solely to His Word for my answers.

Before any progress could be made at all, I knew I'd have to deal with several deeply-rooted ideas which I'd received from the Witnesses. *One* was the idea that the gifts, such as healing, were *only* for the apostolic age. *Another* idea, rooted firmly beside it, said the gifts steadied the toddling, infant church only until it became mature enough to stand by itself; then the gifts were withdrawn. A *third* said that the gifts were used only for confirmation of truth during the period of transition from the Jewish to the Christian economy; the transition was completed when the canon of Scripture was completed, making the gifts unnecessary.

But if the gifts operated only in the presence of the twelve apostles or those on whom they had laid their hands, then what was the scriptural basis for the miracle in my home? I wasn't an apostle, nor had one laid his hands on me! Was it Jesus or the devil who healed Darlene?

Armed with a concordance, a Bible, and a Greek-English Interlinear, I was determined to find the answers for myself. When I began, I had little interest in the person of Jesus as He related to the Trinity, much less in the many different creeds religion had built around Him. But as I followed the Master through the Gospels, we got acquainted. Not only did He come alive, but I uncovered some startling information about the adversary, Satan.

Nowhere could I find any evidence that Satan ever healed anyone, or *wanted* to heal anyone, or ever *would* heal anyone (John 10:10). Jesus, however, came to give abundant life to all who would believe (John 10:10). He did not minister miraculously merely to call attention to His Messiahship; on the contrary, He often told those He healed to keep quiet and refrain from telling anyone Who did it. So it was evident to me that Jesus really cared about the sicknesses and burdens of the people, and was not simply *using* these unfortunate persons to prove a point.

Luke 4:18, 19 opened up a whole new vision of

30

Jesus' ministry for me. I had believed that His primary objective in coming to earth was to "vindicate Jehovah's name." But now I noticed the force of the word *because* in that passage: *"The spirit of the Lord is upon me, because. . . ."* Obviously, all that followed that word would define the purpose of Jesus' ministry, so I read on with great interest: *". . . because he hath anointed me to preach the gospel to the poor; he hath sent me to heal the broken-hearted, to preach deliverance to the captives, and recovering of sight to the blind, to set at liberty them that are bruised, to preach the acceptable year of the Lord."* Not a word about vindicating Jehovah's name! The purpose of Jesus' ministry was to bring us deliverance from all the forces of Satan.

Gradually my eyes were opened. I saw that the supernatural power of Jehovah isn't confined to certain dispensations, but that Jehovah has been working miraculously from the creation of man until now—without letup. His only hindrance is the unbelief of man, primarily among those who call themselves "believers." Nowhere could I continue to justify my unbelief and attribute everything I didn't understand to the devil.

"Lord!" I cried. "Forgive me for making You a liar! You've said one thing in Your Word and I've changed it just as much as Eve changed it, by adding my own 'footnotes.' Help me, Lord! I don't want to doubt You or call You a liar ever again!"

When I began investigating my ideas about the gifts, things really became exciting. First, there was the idea that the apostles held a franchise on the signs and gifts, and that the gifts ceased when they died.

31

Imagine my surprise when I discovered that Paul couldn't be counted as one of the twelve apostles and that there were several *other* apostles named in the New Testament. Momentarily, though, I thought I had a solid Watchtower argument for them: they were "lesser apostles," something like modern missionaries. But it was Paul who eventually helped me over the obstacle.

When choosing an apostle to succeed Judas, Peter stated in Acts 1:21,22 that apostles are *"men which have companied with us all the time that the Lord Jesus went in and out among us, beginning from the baptism of John, unto that same day that he was taken up from us, . . . ordained to be a witness with us of his resurrection."*

In no way could Paul fulfill these qualifications! Furthermore, he didn't even consider himself one of the twelve, though he defended his right to be called an apostle.

Again, in Galatians 1:19, Paul referred to James, the Lord's brother, as one of the apostles. Yet nowhere in the Gospels is the Lord's brother ever listed among the twelve.

When I came to Ephesians 4:8-13, some more of the fog was burned away. First, I noticed that *when Jesus ascended*, He "gave gifts unto men." I wasn't sure which gifts were referred to until I read verse 11: "And he gave some, apostles; and some. . . ." I stopped dead and went back. *After Jesus ascended*, "he gave some *apostles*." But the twelve apostles were appointed *before* the ascension!

Two kinds or groups of apostles? Apparently. One group consisted of the twelve, who were appointed during the earthly ministry of Jesus, to be witnesses of His resurrection. But there are *other* apostles, appointed *after the ascension!*

And what is the mission of these *other* apostles? I found the answer in verse 12: "For the perfecting of the saints, for the work of the ministry, for the edifying of the body of Christ."

Apostles to build up the Body of Christ? Yes, I could see they were certainly needed! But for how long?

I found the answer in verse 13: "Till we all come in the unity of the faith, and of the knowledge of the Son of God, unto a perfect man, unto the measure of the stature of the fulness of Christ."

That blew the lid right off all arguments that the gifts of the Spirit were only for the apostolic age!

"How 'bout that?" I exclaimed. "We're *in* the apostolic age! And if this is true, then we have no logical reason for saying the gifts ceased when the twelve died."

In the hope of finding another area of truth that might further illumine what I had already uncovered, I continued my search.

In Revelation 2:2, I read that Jesus commended the Ephesian church for trying "them which say they are apostles, and are not." I knew that the Lord gave this message to John on Patmos near the end of the first century, after the other apostles had already passed from the scene.

Why would Jesus commend them for *trying* apostles when apostles didn't even exist? It certainly would seem simpler to tell them that there *are* no more apostles and let it go at that. Why *try* something that is nonexistent?

Finally, I cleared the last hurdle when I took a fresh look at 1 Corinthians 13:8-10. This was the passage that the Witnesses quoted repeatedly to prove that the gifts had gone out of existence: *"Charity never faileth: but whether there be prophecies, they shall fail; whether there be tongues, they shall cease; whether there be knowledge, it shall vanish away. For we know in part, and we prophesy in part. But when that which is perfect is come, then that which is in part shall be done away."*

The passage was very familiar to me. Time and again I had quoted it when I wanted to prove that the gifts of the Spirit had passed away. But now I ask if I had been right in assuming that they had *already* passed away.

Paul seemed to answer the question in verse 10: *"But when that which is perfect is come, then that which is in part shall be done away."* I had been taught that the "perfect" thing mentioned here refers to the completed Bible in the hands of the church; once the canon of Scripture was complete and the church was mature, the gifts were no longer needed.

But then I read verse 12, where I found further explanation of the "perfect" thing of verse 10: *"For now we see through a glass, darkly; but then face to face: now I know in part; but then shall I know even as also I am known."*

Suddenly I saw! "That which is perfect" refers to the Church Triumphant when she stands before the Lord face to face—*not* the completed Bible! The Lord is simply saying that we won't need the gifts in heaven!

But there was something else. I had discovered that the word *perfect* in this verse means "mature, or full-grown," and that Paul uses it in reference to

34

men growing up, especially the Body of believers growing up into the fullness of the stature of Christ. So there was every possibility that the gifts *were* given to the infant church only until such a time as she reached maturity.

But from previous studies of the second-century church, I knew full well that, rather than reaching maturity, the church was already well on the road to apostasy. In fact, when Jesus gave His revelation to John, He had to correct the seven churches in Asia for their indifference and disobedience, and for permitting erroneous doctrines and practices in the churches.

Maturity?

No! Rather—unbelief, apostasy in its infant stages, and church organization. No wonder the gifts ceased! Not because the Lord withdrew them, but because there was neither faith nor desire for them. Paul said the gifts came as a result of coveting them, desiring them, and earnestly seeking them. Maturity? Completeness? A full-grown church?

It was now becoming clear!

I saw that *before* the Body could reach full growth and maturity, it must have the gifts Paul mentioned in Ephesians 4:11 and 1 Corinthians 12:7-10, according to what he wrote in 1 Corinthians 12:28-30. How could the church reach maturity without the tools necessary to do it?

My conclusions were:

1. Our Lord did not withdraw the gifts of the Spirit at the end of the apostolic age, simply because there *never was* an end. History also bore this out.

2. The purpose of the gifts of the Spirit was more than authentication, corroboration and substantia-

tion. They were for edification, growth, and ministry. They were the equipment enabling the believer to do the work of the ministry.

So after nearly two months of almost constant searching, praying, and "digging," I finally said to the Lord: "I do believe! If need be, I'll stand alone and let the world laugh at me, but this one thing I know. You're alive and You haven't changed! Further, I'll go back and tell my former brothers that they missed it!"

CHAPTER FOUR

THE DEVIL DID IT!

Nearly three months had passed since the miracle, and "the thing which I greatly feared" (Job 3:25) was about to come upon me. During this deeply satisfying time of soul-searching and systematic Scripture study, I had dropped all my Watchtower activities—the Tuesday night book study, the Friday night Theocratic Ministry school where ministers are trained, and the service meeting where we received actual practice in how to "place" (sell) a Watchtower publication at the front door. On Sunday, I missed the "Tower" study at the hall; but most important to the Society, I missed my field time—the time actually spent going door to door preaching and placing literature.

Eventually I knew I'd receive a visitor from the local congregation, checking up on me. "Are you sick? Have you fallen captive to false doctrines? You aren't losing interest, are you?" Ordinarily, the attention would have been appreciated—but under the circumstances, I almost shuddered, just thinking about it.

Ultimately it happened on a Saturday morning around 10:30. There was a knock at the kitchen door.

"We've got company," I remarked to Glad, as I walked to the door. "Wonder who it could be?"

Something told me to peek out the window before opening the door.

"Glad! It's Lawrence," I whispered urgently. "Get ready!"

Lawrence was one of my closest friends, having helped me build my home. We'd hunted together and spent many hours in the Bible together. Also, he was the local study conductor. Opening the door, I invited him in.

"Hey, man, it's good to see you. Been some time!" I said, smiling and reaching for his hand.

He stepped by me into the kitchen and didn't wait to be seated. His abrupt air signaled that his mission was purely business.

"Where've you been?" he demanded. "We've missed you at the Hall."

"I've been . . . confused," I answered, deliberately controlling my voice and actions lest he sense my nervousness. "Do you remember how Darlene was born with clubfeet?"

"Yes . . . and I'm sorry—but what has that got to do with your being absent?" he replied almost belligerently. Personal views and even friendships have a unique way of being shelved when duties need to be performed.

"Well . . ." I began haltingly, looking directly into his eyes, "Jehovah has healed her!" I stood there saying nothing more and waiting for the explosion I knew would come.

"He did not!" Lawrence shouted angrily. His face was coloring as though he had been insulted. I was aware of his feeling. Whenever a J. W. is

38

doubted, a seething volcano of emotion instantly builds to a bursting point.

"All I know for sure is this," I said, smiling a little wistfully, "whereas she was born crippled, now she is all right."

For a moment he stood there, speechless. Pulling out a chair by the table, I sat down and motioned for him to follow suit, but he refused my offer with a wave of his hand.

"Don't be a fool, Chuck. The devil did it!" he insisted.

"Now wait just a moment. You're a Bible student and a good one. Your Bible says in John 10:10 that the thief comes *only* to steal, destroy, and kill," I explained slowly and gently, hoping to blunt his hostility. "If it was the devil who healed my baby, then he isn't so bad after all!" It just slipped out, unpremeditated. I now understood exactly what Solomon meant in Proverbs, when he spoke of the impossibility of taking back spent words.

Without saying another word, Lawrence whirled around and stomped out of the house, leaving the door wide open behind him. Outside, I could hear his spinning tires as he roared out of the yard. Without watching him, I knew he wasn't bothering to look back. I also knew this wouldn't be the last I'd hear of the matter. He would make a complete report to the Congregational Servant at the Kingdom Hall. He would undoubtedly say that "Brother Trombley has been deceived into thinking Jehovah healed his daughter and consequently has fallen into error." Because he hadn't taken time to hear the whole account, his explanation would be confusing.

39

More than two weeks passed while Glad and I continued some door-to-door witnessing, presenting all the old Watchtower teachings, plus a few new ideas about healing! I avoided the Kingdom Hall, however. Then one noon, Glad went out to check the mail box. "Chuck," she called when she returned to the house, "there's a letter here from Dr. Lee. Did you remember to pay him?"

"Come to think of it, I forgot," I confessed. "I'll go right in and take care of it. Give me the bill!"

When I opened the envelope, however, there was no bill inside. Instead, I found a neat, typewritten note which read something like this:

"If we are going to do anything for your daughter, the treatment must be done while she is small. I appreciate the fact that it is expensive, but we can arrange it on a time payment basis if you prefer. But please bring the child in. Thank you."

Now here was a new twist of events. Explaining the acts of God to a religionist who doesn't believe is *one* thing—but a medical practitioner? Well . . . that's a different story. At least the religionist accepts the fact of God, but does a doctor? Somehow I had the idea then that all doctors lived in their own private world of unbelief. (I have since found that there are many who have great faith.)

After a healthy discussion, Glad volunteered to write Dr. Lee and explain what had happened. I was supposed to be the head of my home, but I was genuinely relieved to pass that responsibility on to my wife. She wrote a nice letter of explanation, enclosed a tract by Oral Roberts entitled "If You Need Healing, Do These Things," and asked for a full, final bill. After praying together while we held

40

the envelope between us, we asked God to help him understand.

His answer came by return mail. Enclosed was the bill for fifteen dollars but across the front was stamped: "Paid in Full."

We've often wondered what went on in his mind and why he canceled the bill. Did he believe our testimony? Or did he think we were country bumpkins or crackpots, better left alone? I prefer to believe the best, but—do doctors cancel their bills and mark them "Paid in Full"?

I knew what the Witnesses would say: If the devil healed Darlene, then no doubt he also paid the bill!

CHAPTER FIVE

THE CLOSING GATES
OF THE KINGDOM

It was a moody Thursday afternoon the following week. The late winter sky had a sinister gray look and the leafless trees stood as silent as sentries guarding a tomb.

Work was slow at the shoe factory where I worked. I was at home, lounging around and reading, when there was a firm knock on the front door.

When I opened the door I was confronted by two men. I recognized one as the Congregational Servant from the Kingdom Hall, but the other was a total stranger.

"Come in, brothers. This is a surprise," I lied. They had been expected since the day Lawrence stormed from the house and reported me as a traitor to the Organization.

They stepped inside, nodding in response to my greeting. Trying to appear confident and at ease, I took their coats and laid them neatly on the bed. When I returned to the living room, I found Glad standing there with a questioning look.

"Honey, this is Tony DiNardo from the Hall and . . . ?" my voice trailed off, leaving opportunity for the minister to introduce the other man.

"This is Frank Marsh, the District Servant."

In Protestant circles he would be called a district superintendent or bishop. His position was an influential one, and he was a direct representative of the Society in Brooklyn; the Congregational Servant was the minister of the local congregation.

After shaking our hands limply but politely, the two men seated themselves side by side on the sofa, leaving Glad and me the two chairs across the room. At their feet I noticed the familiar brown briefcases, often referred to as "portable ammunition dumps." Inside would be several different Bible translations, including the Society's *New World Translation*, a copy of *Make Sure Of All Things* (the J. W. concordance), an ample supply of Watchtower tracts and "The Tower."

I felt uneasy and I was sure it was evident. My mouth was dry and I held my hands together to steady them. Glancing aside toward Glad, I sensed her own anxiety. Neither of us had anything to fear physically, but the psychological intimidation was even worse. I mutely waited for them to open the conversation.

"Mr. Trombley," DiNardo began (the term "brother" had already been dropped), "I've received a complaint that you were belligerent to a brother when he was only trying to finish his assignment and check on your faithfulness to Jehovah's Organization."

My first impulse was to set him straight, but I felt a check. Better wait and see what Lawrence had reported.

"We want to be fair, so we'd like to hear *your* side of the story. Jehovah demands a clean organization, you know," he said, lifting his eyebrows.

There wasn't any trace of a smile on his face—only blankness, which I interpreted as part of his psychological attack.

"You tell me exactly what the complaint is and I'll either plead innocent or guilty or offer an explanation," I suggested, making sure my voice was kept low.

"The report is that you claim Jehovah healed your infant daughter's clubfeet, and when you were corrected about this false assumption and given the Bible truth about it, you responded in a non-Christian way. Is this true?" he inquired.

He reached into his bag and pulled out the faded green book which I recognized as the Watchtower Bible. His actions alerted me that he was prepared for an instant rebuttal, regardless of what I said.

"If you mean I told Lawrence that Jehovah healed my daughter, you're perfectly right. He did!" I declared. "And I also told Lawrence that it was impossible for me to retract my position. However, he did *not* prove to me from Scripture that I was wrong."

I excused myself and walked across the room to my desk, where I picked up my Bible.

"If Lawrence reported the incident exactly as it happened, then he told you I also said that, according to John 10:10, the thief comes *only* to hurt, destroy and kill. Furthermore, I told Lawrence that if it was the devil who healed my daughter, then he wasn't so bad after all. Did he tell you I said that?" I didn't wait for his answer but continued: "We didn't get to discuss anything further, because he left immediately, madder than a wet hen."

"You can't really believe in healing, after the thorough teaching you've received," the District

Servant said sarcastically. Holding his Bible toward me like a pointer, he said, "We've exposed *that* false doctrine long ago!"

Lowering his arm, he sat back with a smug look on his face. Tension continued to build as we balanced and counterbalanced our positions. The two men were attentive when I explained my newfound faith and my absolute certainty that Jehovah had made Himself known to me through this miracle of healing; but it soon became obvious that their polite attention was a prearranged tactic. By feigning interest in my arguments and letting me talk, they were hoping I'd put my foot in my own mouth. I saw this very clearly, and realized they weren't "bear-hunting with a willow switch."

"My daughter who was once crippled is now healed!" I insisted. "Are *you* men ready to make a definite, eternal evaluation that Jehovah God had absolutely nothing to do with this healing and renounce it entirely as the work of Satan? Are you ready to make that decision, knowing full well the possibility—that if you're wrong, you're guilty of blasphemy? You know the eternal consequences of that. Will you do that?"

Suddenly I felt as bold as a prophet. But before I was able to force an answer or continue, they switched subjects. I knew then that they were "running." This is an old Watchtower ploy; if used skillfully, it can often get you out of an embarrassing situation.

"Is it true your in-laws were once Jehovah's Witnesses?" Marsh asked.

"Yes, that's true," I replied, but added nothing more. I wanted to draw them out completely and see exactly what they were after.

"Why did they leave the Society?"

Now I perceived their modus operandi. They were using the practiced tactics of a trial lawyer. By asking certain questions, they were hoping to maneuver me into a position where they could spring the trapdoor and let me hang myself. Cautiously I reinforced my guard on both my tongue and my mind.

"They left because the late Judge Rutherford closed heaven to all except the 144,000* when he established the New World Society.† Quite frankly, they couldn't find any solid truth in such an idea. Rutherford said the Holy Spirit had been withdrawn from all except "the remnant"—that is, any of the 144,000 still living. (Note: The J. W.'s have again changed this point of doctrine and are now teaching that the earthbound Witnesses can have a measure of the Spirit even though they *are* not and *can* not be born again.)

"You see," I continued, "Papa had been with the Society since 1914 and had watched this change emerge. He felt there wasn't any Bible basis for such extremism, and when his sons were refused the Communion elements during a Memorial Supper, he simply walked out and left the Society."

"Did he consider his sons as part of the remnant?" DiNardo asked, raising his voice.

---

* According to J. W. teaching, the 144,000 are all the Christian believers who lived from Pentecost until 1914. They are the Body of Christ, the true church—the only ones who can be born again and Spirit-filled.

† According to Rutherford, only the 144,000 can enter heaven. But all other J. W.'s can become members of Jehovah's *New World Society*, which is the spiritual organization destined to become God's Kingdom *on earth*.

46

"They had all had real experiences with the Lord and each of them bore the marks of one whose nature had been changed. Is it impossible for young people today to be a part of the remnant?" I asked.

Without bothering to answer my question, they continued *their* questioning, lest I divert them.

"And have you been fellowshipping with them?" the District Servant asked.

This question, I instantly realized, was intended to intimidate me further. Jehovah's Witnesses aren't allowed any contact with those who have left the Society or who have been excommunicated for any reason.

Without waiting for my reply, Marsh continued, his voice more commanding. "You know that according to Matthew 24:48, your in-laws are 'evil servants,' having left the true body of Jehovah's Witnesses. You can't have anything to do with them! Over the years many have gone back from the truth and become entangled with Babylon."

I tried to interrupt and explain that Papa had never done or said anything against the Society, but he wouldn't listen.

"And didn't he start another sect in competition with the Society, called the Christian Family Circle?"

"Yes, sir! We have been fellowshipping with them—but no, sir, he did *not* start another sect. The CFC is a family group—no more! It is made up of our family—and friends—and nowhere in Scripture does it forbid family fellowships, providing they are neither ungodly, nor unbelievers, nor heathen. Papa's only fault was daring to disagree

47

with Judge Rutherford's doctrine—and Judge Rutherford has been proven wrong on several counts *since!*"

"Wrong? What do you mean?" they demanded, both speaking at the same time.

This was a sore spot with the Organization and I intended to expose it fully.

"I'm sorry. He was more than wrong; he was a modern false prophet! He prophesied that the ancient worthies from Abel to the last Old Testament prophet would be resurrected and return to earth as human beings in 1925. In fact, the judge even built a palatial mansion in San Diego, which he called Beth Sarim, for them to live in. When they didn't show, the judge lived there himself until his death. Can anyone deny that?"

"Well. . . ." one of them tried to explain.

"Let me finish, please," I said. "Deuteronomy 18:22 says that if a person speaks in the name of Jehovah and it doesn't come to pass, then Jehovah has not spoken. If I remember right, it was on September 25, 1920, that Rutherford gave his lecture, "Millions Now Living Shall Never Die," and in it predicted a resurrection of all dead Witnesses. He said that all Adamic death would end at the moment of this resurrection, and no more funeral wreaths would be hanging from doors. The records show that the Society sold the property in 1942, after his death, in hopes that his name and his false prophecies would soon be forgotten."

I knew they would dodge this embarrassing subject and pounce on me from another angle at the first opportunity—and I was determined to hold them to the issue until something was settled. Hardly pausing for breath, I plunged on.

48

"Papa was a candid and honest man. When 1925 passed and nothing happened, he watched Rutherford skillfully switch the emphasis to door-to-door work.

Papa was aware that our founder, Pastor Charles Taze Russell, had also made predictions that failed. As late as 1907 he said that *if* 1915 passed without the elect's being resurrected and natural Israel's being restored, then his chronology would be proven wrong. He predicted that the Kingdom of God would crush the Gentile image in 1915, and the great tribulation would *end* then." I purposely went into some detail to make sure they understood what I was saying, and also in the hope that if they hadn't seen these gross inconsistencies before, they would now.

"And did any of these things come to pass?" I waited, pressing for an answer. They stared blankly at me.

"Not one point of the prophecies made by Rutherford and Russell came to pass," I went on. "Yet the Society continues to accept most of their doctrines as gospel. Isn't this dangerous, brothers?" I asked.

One of them mumbled something about approaching greater light. I certainly hadn't anticipated any such involvement when they entered the house about an hour ago, but it was impossible to retreat now.

Changing the subject again, DiNardo said, "I understand your in-laws teach that the Society is wrong in preaching the good news that we are the true Israel of God. Don't they teach a literal regathering of the Jews back to Palestine?"

The answer to that question was well known.

Papa had written study booklets emphasizing this truth; but these men were apparently not aware that Rutherford had changed this doctrine from the way Russell taught it originally, although each man claimed to be Jehovah's channel of communication through which new truth was dispensed. This was only one of some 148 doctrinal changes that took place under Rutherford's leadership.

"I'm glad you brought that up," I said. "Turn in your Bibles to Romans, chapter eleven. There are several remarkable truths in verses 25 through 32. Number one is in verse 25, where Paul says the true Israel of God has been blinded *until* the time of the Gentiles is finished—which is, of course, Armageddon. Right? In verse 27 I see that Israel won't have her sins removed until *after* the Deliverer from Zion comes in. In verse 28, they, Israel, are shown to be *enemies of the Gospel*, for the sake of the Gentile Christians. Finally, in verse 32, God concludes them (Israel) *all in unbelief*.

"Putting all this together logically, some pertinent questions arise. If the Society *is* true Israel, as it claims to be, then isn't it walking in blindness? And won't it continue to walk that way until Armageddon? If it is Israel, isn't it an enemy of the Gospel? And hasn't God set it aside in unbelief? *If the society is the true Israel, then this is the only logical conclusion anyone can come to. What do you say?"

Marsh seemed agitated that I would even dare suggest such an interpretation; he colored visibly.

"If, as Papa taught, Israel is the *natural* Jew," I added, "then a natural restoration of the nation is not only possible but probable."

Something had happened within me. Nothing I

50

said was deliberately planned. I realized now that the Holy Spirit had taken over and infused me with a new surge of wisdom. Still speaking softly and confidently, I concluded, "Perhaps this is the reason so many earnest people in the Society seem to be blinded to real Bible truths like healing and the supernatural. Jesus isn't dead, or dissolved into gases, or preserved in heaven as a memorial, as Russell and Rutherford taught. He's alive, and Glad and I have some living evidence to prove it!"

Without waiting for their reaction I turned to Glad. "Go get the baby and let them see a genuine miracle!"

She got up and disappeared into the bedroom. Turning back toward the two officials, I continued with a statement of my beliefs.

"I've satisfied myself that Russell was wrong on at least two points: miracles haven't ceased and Jesus did not return in 1874.* Rutherford also established himself as an unreliable teacher when he predicted the resurrection in 1925 and it failed to materialize. It has become increasingly difficult for me to accept the Society as the administrator of Jehovah's Kingdom, with all its inconsistencies and changeable doctrines.

"To me, the Bible seems very definite that apostles and prophets, as well as healings and other supernatural gifts, will not be removed until the church is caught up to heaven. Henceforth, I've committed myself to believing the Bible exactly as it is written, without resorting to outside study aids to guide my thinking. Quite frankly, I feel that the

* When Russell's prediction did not come true, the Organization quickly suppressed all talk of the error, and began to talk of 1914 as the key date.

51

Society has robbed me, but I fully intend to regain every promise the Word says is mine!"

My defense was finished. There wasn't anything I could add that would help or jeopardize my case. They had been listening, but certainly were not hearing.

DiNardo started to speak. "You realize that, without Jehovah's study helps, you can't receive proper meat in due season. Only through these helps is divine truth given. It's impossible to arrive at the truth or keep the truth without them."

He didn't sound angry, just frustrated. Our attention suddenly turned to Glad as she entered the room with the baby.

"See those feet?" I said, pointing to them. "They're perfectly normal. Look at them! Who did that? Jesus or the devil? Does something as beautiful as that look like the work of the devil?"

"Mr. Trombley, were you ever baptized as one of Jehovah's Witnesses?" DiNardo asked calmly, avoiding the question.

"I was baptized as a Bible student," I explained. "If, at that time, I understood the meaning of baptism and dedication by immersion, and if my life was one of consecrated service to Jehovah, would *you* say I was baptized?"

"You know the truth," DiNardo cautioned me, "and you'll have to answer to Jehovah for the rejection of His Organization. There isn't any other way to survive the Armageddon holocaust; there isn't any other means of salvation outside His Theocratic Organization. You know that!"

"No! I don't know that," I countered. "Not any longer. I *do* know the Society is wrong in several very important matters. I personally feel it is wisdom to reexamine the whole system. Don't you teach that bad fruits identify a religious organization? If the clergy of Christendom, with their liberal attitudes and unbelief, reflect the evil of their organizations, can't the Society be judged by the same principle? For this reason, I have reached a conclusion: I *must* reject the Society until further notice. Nothing else would be honest."

DiNardo put his Bible back in his bag. "The Society wants to be honest also," he said. "We admit our past mistakes, but our knowledge will be increased as the light grows brighter. It isn't fair for you to judge the Society and its present truth within the framework of Russell and Rutherford!"

Instinctively I knew the afternoon's conversation was rapidly coming to a close.

"We must go now. We have some more calls to make."

"But fellows," I challenged while waiting for Glad to return with their coats, "Russell and Rutherford were just as sure as you are. You're still preaching their major doctrines; you're still denying healing; you're still teaching that the gifts are nonexistent; you're still denying the physical resurrection of Jesus, and His literal second coming."

"We must be going," one of them insisted as they reached for their coats.

"Can't you see that the real issue is whether the devil or Jesus healed my daughter? That's the issue and I cannot, I simply will not deny what Jesus did! If this means my disfellowshipping, then so be it. I regret it, but I cannot deny what God has done. To do so would be blasphemy, and I'd rather fear God than the threats and judgments of the Society."

Helping them on with their coats, I added sincerely, "I appreciate your interest in my spiritual welfare and your stopping by. There's only one desire in my heart—that all my brothers in the Society could know the living Christ in His power as I do. Would you care to have prayer with us before you leave?" I asked.

"No, we can't do that!" they stammered in unison.

Then, without looking back, they walked toward their car. I could see one nod his head in response to a remark made by the other. It wasn't hard to guess the tenor of their conversation.

Closing the door, I turned to Glad and said with finality, "That's that! Where do we go from here?"

She tilted her head, shrugged her shoulders, and gave me one of her understanding looks.

"It'll be a long time before we'll know the full effect of this afternoon," I mused. "Whatever the effect, it won't be nice, but I still feel good. Did we ever have a better opportunity to stand for Jesus?"

Suddenly my knees began to feel weak, and I crossed the room and dropped into a chair. For the first time, I was aware of how upset I had been, even though I had mentally prepared myself for the confrontation that had just taken place.

Theoretically, we had been informally kicked out of the Kingdom of God. One who questioned the Society as I had didn't come out smelling like a rose. We would be given the cold shoulder and the silent treatment by those we knew in the Organization. Undoubtedly, we'd lose our personal friends. They would all be publicly forbidden to talk with us or have any fellowship with us. We were now "evil servants," fit only for destruction.

Out across the valley, edged by the window frame, Bald Hill looked as lonely as I now felt. There wasn't any sign of wildlife, not even the sound of a distant automobile. Nothing—except the mournful cry of a crow. We were completely alone.

CHAPTER SIX

"IT'S ONLY EMOTIONALISM"

The next few weeks were difficult. Word soon spread throughout the shoe factory that "Trombley has *really* flipped on religion." When I was a Witness, they had tolerated me as an oddball; but now the real pressure began.

One must understand New Englanders, and especially Vermonters, to appreciate their wariness of emotion. Spiritually, New England was the birth place of Universalism, Unitarianism, liberalism and formalism. Most New Englanders do not appreciate any public display of religion, much less witnessing about a personal experience. Anyone a bit more religious than the average churchgoer is branded a fanatic—and that's the way *I* was branded. It hurt, but I was determined to stand for what I believed.

One Monday morning, shortly after I arrived at work, I passed a machine operated by the daughter of a friend of ours.

"Chuck!" Marie called to me above the rasping noise of the wood lathes, saws and planers. "Have you ever heard anything about the baptism in the Holy Spirit?"

"What's with her?" I wondered. Picking up one of the maple heels she was grading, I tossed it back and forth between my hands like a toy.

"Some," I said. "I've read about it a little." (Watchtower theology says that only the 144,000 can be baptized in the Holy Spirit, and the Society emphasizes that the Holy Spirit is not a person, but only God's active *force*.) "Why do you ask?"

Marie knew about Darlene's miracle but hadn't ever declared her position, either pro or con.

"Oh, just asking," she replied. "By the way," she shouted above the shrill noise, "would you like to come to a Bible meeting tonight? There'll be a visiting speaker."

"Sure. Sounds good. Where and what time?"

"Starts at 7:30. Here's the address in Claremont."

Marie scratched the address on a piece of yellow order paper and handed it to me, after making me promise I'd be there. Walking back to my lathe, I wondered about her sudden interest in Bible meetings. What I visualized was a "spiritual jam session," where several Bible students would gather around a table or in a living room, and cross Bible swords with the visiting speaker, halting the battle just short of a vicious argument. The Witnesses often played these Bible games, which provided unlimited opportunities to argue points of doctrine under pressure. Although it was rare that anyone conceded a point, it did give us battle-front conditions in which we shored up our beliefs. Furthermore, these debates were fun, unless someone got "shoutin' mad."

Later I discovered that Marie had deliberately avoided telling me what kind of meeting she was inviting me to, because she had been converted in one of those meetings just two weeks earlier and was hoping the same thing would happen to me.

She was wise: had I known it was a revival meeting, I'd have turned down her invitation.

That evening I told Glad about the meeting, and she said she wanted to come along. After leaving Darlene and David with Mother Allen, we drove the eighteen miles to Claremont. The address was on a back street in the Polish section of town and we had difficulty finding it.

When we finally arrived, I noticed several older cars parked in front of a long, narrow building that was badly in need of paint. It looked like just another of the many abandoned and unused churches in Vermont. In the front yard, I noticed a small, hand-painted sign, faded and peeled, but still readable:

PENTECOSTAL CHURCH
Dan Cornelius, Pastor

Leaving the security of the car, we climbed the three wooden steps that led to the stoop. When I opened the door, I was greeted by a sight I'd never seen before.

There were about 50 theater-type seats on each side of a long aisle, and about half of them were filled with people. The auditorium itself was completely unadorned except for a huge sign over the platform which read: HOLINESS UNTO THE LORD.

"Well, that's appropriate," I thought. "Jehovah is holy! But why are these people so afraid of using His true name, Jehovah?"

We slipped unnoticed into two empty seats in the

back row, feeling quite out of place in this obviously Russian congregation.

A young man was speaking (in English, fortunately!), whom I assumed was the visiting speaker Marie had mentioned. (Another man was seated on the platform—probably the pastor.) The evangelist was dressed in a plain black suit with a white shirt and black tie. Urged on by spontaneous "amens" and "hallelujahs" from the congregation, he thundered out his message. His tie was loosened, and his hands flayed the air. I thought of Abraham Lincoln's remark that, if he had to listen to a preacher, he wanted one who acted as though he were fighting a swarm of bees. He would have appreciated this young man.

I don't remember a word he said; I was too engrossed in studying his delivery. How different this was from my Watchtower training! In ministry school, we had been taught to control our voices, to speak slowly and distinctly, to stand erect with our toes at a 45 degree angle, and never, never to swing our arms.

But this fellow broke *all* the rules! He shouted until his face grew red and the veins of his neck stood out. He gestured wildly with one hand and waved a white handkerchief in the other. He worked so hard at his sermon that the sweat ran down the sides of his face. Meanwhile, the congregation listened spellbound, utterly absorbed in what he was saying.

"I don't know what this is all about, but they sure are emotional," I thought.

Then I noticed Marie, who had invited me to this meeting. She sat only two rows from the front and I could read her lips saying, "Amen."

"I'll have to talk with her tomorrow," I mused. "She acts like she enjoys all this—but why did she invite me?"

The service was strange and quite unlike anything I'd ever attended before. What a departure from the quiet, refined conduct cherished by the staid Vermonter, and how far removed from the lifeless meetings at the Kingdom Hall!

During the preaching service, a strange thing happened. On the other side of the church, a short, gray-haired woman stood up. She had on a long black coat and a little black hat perched on top of her head. She raised her right arm straight up, and immediately that shouting preacher descended from the jetstream where he had been carried along and stopped talking. The instant silence unnerved me even more. I remember thinking, "He can't be *too* fanatical; at least he has control of his shouting."

Then the little woman began speaking in a strange language of some kind that I'd never heard before. Her voice was high and shrill, and she spoke very rapidly.

I leaned toward my wife. "What on earth is she doing?" I whispered. "Laying an egg?"

Glad looked at me and lifted her eyebrows as if to say, "Who knows?"

I glanced across the church at Marie and noticed that she was studying me with a quizzical expression. It was obvious that she was wondering about my reactions.

If I could have enlightened her right then, it would have been short and sour: "Pure emotionalism and unnecessary fanaticism!"

Then another strange thing happened! From

somewhere on my side of the building, a man's voice boomed, "Thus saith the Lord. . . ."

He was a big man, somewhat taller than those around him. His voice sounded powerful and authoritative. He said something about God being in that place to save a lost, self-righteous sinner.

Partially ducking my head, I looked around furtively. The other members of the congregation seemed to have their eyes closed, waiting for something to happen. When he finished, many of the people said "Amen" and "Praise the Lord!"

Almost the instant he stopped talking, the evangelist was off and running again as though he had never been interrupted. The delay hadn't cooled his ardor at all.

But what did that man mean, "Thus saith the Lord"? Was he trying to say something for Jehovah?

The evangelist finally finished and asked the congregation to stand. Then he began an appeal for sinners to come forward. No one responded. Next he pleaded for *the* sinner to come. Still no one moved. Then he changed his approach and asked those who needed more holiness to come. Still, nothing.

After that, he called for those who wanted the baptism of the Holy Ghost—but again, no one left his seat. Finally, in desperation, he asked *everyone* to come and pray for revival.

At first, no one moved. Then slowly, one by one, the worshipers rose to their feet and walked to the front of the church. Meanwhile the pianist was playing some background music, soft and slow—hindering rather than encouraging people to respond quickly.

The first ones reaching the front knelt at the altar rail; the others knelt wherever they found room.

Then, like an orchestra tuning up, they started praying—some in English, others in Russian, but all at the same time. Glad and I stood conspicuously alone at the back of the building. If there is anything more embarrassing or lonely than walking the aisle of a church to make a public confession of Christ, it is having the whole church go to the altar to pray and leaving you standing alone in the pews.

The noise got louder and louder. I squirmed nervously and looked at Glad for consolation. Never in our lives had we read of, heard about, or seen anything quite like this. What were Jehovah's Witnesses doing in a place like this?

Then the pastor noticed us. Slipping from his chair on the platform, he started walking straight toward us. Not knowing what to expect, I folded my arms and moved just slightly in front of Glad, as though to protect her. He stopped about three feet in front of us and asked me, "Are you a minister?"

"Uh-oh, here we go again," I thought. "When he discovers who and what we are, he'll ask us to leave—pronto."

Throwing my shoulders back and drawing in a deep breath, I said, "Yes, sir. I'm one of Jehovah's Witnesses."

Reaching out with his right hand and grasping mine, he smiled warmly. "God bless you. I'm glad you're here!"

"You are?" I thought to myself. He stood there beaming at us as though he really meant it!

"Thank you!" I smiled feebly, slipping my hand into Glad's arm, and pulling her toward the door. "Thank you again . . . We must go now . . . Bye . . ."

After we were safely sheltered in the privacy of our car I said, "Have you ever seen anything like that?"

"No, and I hope we don't ever again," Glad replied.

We started the long drive home, and for a while neither of us said a word. I'm sure we were both sifting out what we had heard and seen. Finally I broke the silence.

"I'll never go back there again. How about you?"

"Are you kidding?" she said. Her tone of voice let me know that the whole scene had been utterly distasteful to her.

By the time we reached Bellows Falls, however, I had mulled the situation over more thoroughly and my curiosity was coming alive again. "I wonder if they're like that *all* the time," I mused. "Might be interesting to go again, just to see."

CHAPTER SEVEN

"IT'S YOUR DECISION"

Next morning at work I looked for Marie, but she found me first. Ordinarily she was somewhat reserved, but this morning she almost danced toward me.

"Chuck, what did you think of the meeting?"

Turning to punch the time clock, I pursed my lips, took a deep breath, and waited a moment before answering. "Marie, I don't want to hurt your feelings, but don't you think the whole thing is, well . . . odd? What do *you* think of all that emotionalism? And what about that woman speaking in that funny language? Surely you don't believe God wants us to do that *today!*"

"Why not?" she replied. "They spoke in tongues in Bible times."

"But there's very little explanation of tongues in the Bible, Marie. If God wanted us to speak in tongues, why didn't He give us more information?"

"Why don't you read the book of Acts again?" she suggested with a smile. "Maybe there's more information there than you think."

I walked to my machine, hoping the noise of the lathe would drown out any further conversation;

but the more I sought to forget her comments, the more insistent they became. Before the morning was over, I had a real argument going with myself.

My background said that the baptism in the Spirit was only for the 144,000 called the "little flock." It was received by them when they were "born again" to heavenly hopes and aspirations. But the power associated with the experience as recorded in Acts was only for launching the infant church until it became more mature.

It hadn't yet dawned on me that the same scriptures that unraveled the healing controversy could have solved this question also. Unknowingly I had bypassed the tongues issue.

During my lunch hour, I retreated to my car, took Marie's advice, and read through the book of Acts. She was right. There was considerably more about tongues-speaking than I had realized. And I did observe the enthusiasm and excitement of the early church which seemed to be missing from our congregations today.

After supper that night, I persuaded Glad to go back with me into the "land of dangerous living." The service was much like that of the previous evening. At the close of his message, the evangelist used the same methods we had seen the night before—but this time we were prepared for him. When he asked the people to stand, we remained seated, safely hidden behind the people standing in front of us. Both the evangelist and the pastor were busy, and for a while they completely ignored us.

Working together as a team, they prayed for the people who went forward, laying their hands on each head and praying in that strange language that

Marie called "tongues." Meanwhile Glad and I held hands for mutual security, and occasionally gave each other questioning looks.

While we were sitting there watching, the pastor came back and invited Glad and me to his home. Seeing an opportunity to get some of our questions answered, we accepted his invitation.

Later, while sitting around his kitchen table drinking too many cups of coffee and eating too many cookies, we "grilled" him about the things we had seen in the meetings, as well as his views on healing, a burning hell, a "God with three heads," and life after death.

"Pastor Dan, do you believe in healing and apostles for today?" I inquired.

"Of course. Our movement has always believed in the gifts of the Spirit," he answered. Immediately I felt some rapport with him. I knew that I wasn't standing alone with the truths I had recently discovered in the Word.

"If you believe in these marvelous truths, why have you kept them hidden for so long?" I asked him. "Why aren't your people going from door to door telling everyone about these wonderful things?"

"That's the weak link in our chain," Dan apologetically replied.

When I questioned him about a burning hell and other controversial issues, he'd smile warmly and say, "Oh, is that what you believe? God bless you!" After a few responses like this, I was wondering if he was normal.

"What's wrong with him?" I asked Gladys after we left. "How can I lead him into the real truth when all he does is grin and say 'God bless you'?"

I've since learned that Dan was under the anointing and control of the Spirit of Jesus that night. Actually I was experiencing Christ in him. I found out later that Dan's normal nature is one that thrives on "heated" Bible discussions, and I've been in several with him. Dan didn't know it then, but the Spirit was leading him in the only effective method of winning a cultist to Christ. Both Glad and I were impressed by Dan's gracious, low-key approach, and we decided to continue attending the special services at his church.

That month of meetings in the little Russian church both blessed and bothered me. I knew I had the right doctrine, but these folk seemed to have the right spirit. As a result, my nights became wide-awake nightmares; my overloaded brain wouldn't let me sleep. I was engaged in a huge wrestling match with my own soul. Time after time I cried, "Where is the answer, God?" In desperation, I decided to have another talk with the pastor.

"Dan, I'm confused and need help." I poured out my heart to him, confiding in him all the unanswered questions that had grown out of weeks of confused anxiety. "My desire is to genuinely know the Lord. Not just know *about* Him; I want to *know* Him!"

"Chuck," Dan asked, "have you accepted Jesus as your Savior yet?" That was the last question in the world I expected. I had anticipated some discussion about how God healed, or an attempt to justify the strange doctrines—but this? I mulled it over for a second or two.

"Of course," I answered almost indignantly. "I've taught the Bible, preached to others, placed

67

many pieces of literature, and done my best to obey the Bible. That isn't my problem. . . ."

"That isn't what I asked, "Dan insisted. "Have *you* . . . no . . . let me put it this way, Chuck—" He slowed his voice, saying each word distinctly. "When . . . and . . . where . . . did you invite Jesus as God and Savior into your life? When did you receive His nature into your soul?"

There was silence in the room. My reaction to his question was largely negative; but at the same time I felt a strong urge to answer him. Why was he so intent on making Jesus God? And how can you receive something into your soul when you *are* a soul? His steady look made me feel uncomfortable, but I intuitively knew he wasn't trying to trap me.

"Well, I've always believed in Jesus Christ and God His Father, so I'm certainly not an unbeliever. Is that what you're after?"

My words sounded empty and hollow in my own ears. Why couldn't I pinpoint what he wanted, and why couldn't he understand my problem?

"Hold it a moment, Chuck! You're trying to approach Jesus through your mind and you're avoiding my question. This is very important, if you want me to help you—and I believe I can. When did you actually ask Jesus Christ to come into your life and take control?" Leaning back, he crossed his legs and waited for me to answer, as though he knew it would take me some time to explain.

I wanted help—didn't he realize that? But I didn't want his religion. All the excessive demonstration and emotionalism didn't really frighten me, but it *did* bother me and turn me off. And I couldn't find any way to identify with their dark-age doctrines.

"Dan," I tried to explain, "I was baptized when I was thirteen and dedicated my life to God the best I knew how. Since then I've studied and taken in knowledge of God."

"But Chuck," Dan interrupted, "making Jesus your Lord can't be done through the intellect or learning the Bible!" Turning in his chair he reached for the Bible on the table beside him. "One of the peculiarities of Christianity is that you must experience it first—something you may not fully understand—and then the understanding will follow."

Turning in his Bible, he read from 1 Corinthians 2:14: *"But the natural man receiveth not the things of the Spirit of God: . . . neither can he know them, because they are spiritually discerned."*

"You see," he said, "you come to Jesus first; and after He is Lord of your life, the Spirit will lead you into the understanding of your experiences. It's called the walk of faith. You trust Him for what you don't understand. That's why I didn't ask you when *you* gave yourself to Him, but when you asked *Him* to come into your life."

The room was gravely silent again. I had learned to appreciate this man sitting before me with his open Bible, but I felt that he was pushing me now.

Lowering my head, I said, "I don't know, Dan. I just don't know."

"Just take your time and think it through," he replied. "It's your decision and it's your life."

CHAPTER EIGHT

I'M ONE OF THE 144,000

How long I sat there, I don't know. For endless moments I was completely submerged in serious thought about Dan's question. *When did Jesus Christ come into my life?* What did Dan want, a date? I sat there trying to recall some vivid experience that I could say was "the time" when Christ came into my life. But my mind was completely blank.

Dan was still sitting motionless across from me. Finally I looked at him and said, "Dan, I just don't know. If He ever came into my life, I don't know when it was."

I felt both embarrassed and disturbed to make this admission. What kind of Bible student was I, claiming to have all the truth and then saying, "I don't know"? And to a preacher of Christendom who didn't have the truth!

"Chuck," Dan said quietly, "if you're not sure when Jesus came into your life, then there's a good chance you've never asked Him in. Why don't you get that matter cleared up, and see if this isn't the answer to your problem? Okay?"

"But what should I do? I'm not quite sure I understand."

He laid both his hands, palms down, on his

Bible. "It's all right here, Chuck. Confess Jesus as Lord, and let Him forgive your sins. Stop trying to please Him or earn His favors. Tell Him you'll be His disciple and His witness. Then invite Him into your life and ask Him to take over. Try it!"

Having thoroughly prepared the soil of my heart, he walked out to the kitchen and left the harvest to the Lord. He must have sensed my embarrassment and desire to be alone.

For once, my mind was quiet. Dan's words kept burning in my ears: "When did you ask Him to come into your life?"

When did I? I'd assumed everything was all right with Jehovah and me. I believed in Jesus, didn't I? I thought so, but now I wasn't so sure.

In my training, the emphasis had been on being a witness for Jehovah, who alone was the true God. I knew that Jesus, whom we called Jehovah's *created* son,* had died on the cross; but was He my *Lord*? I couldn't remember that anyone had ever asked me such a personal question before, nor was it one we discussed at the Kingdom Hall. After all, the vindication of Jehovah's name was the most important thing, and Jesus' work on the cross was secondary.

But from somewhere deep within my subconsciousness came a thought: "Isn't it possible for you to master all knowledge possible *about* a person and still not know him?"

"Yes!" I reasoned. "That's possible."

Then another thought surfaced: "You've taught about Jesus' creation, where He came from, what

---

* J. W.'s view Jesus both as Jehovah's created son, and as the first created angel; in fact, they consider all angels to be "sons of God."

He did, and even the exact hour of His death; but do you *know* Him? Really?"

The answer to that question was all too clear: I couldn't honestly say I *knew* Him, in the sense of having a personal relationship with Him.

"Dear God," I prayed silently, "Help me! I'm more mixed up than before."

In desperation, I picked up my J. W. Bible and turned to the most comforting passage I knew—the fourteenth chapter of John. When I came to the seventh verse, I stopped dead:

> *If you had known me, you should have known my Father also: and from henceforth you have seen him and known him.*

That verse mystified me! It seemed to suggest that one couldn't know the Father without first knowing Jesus. But that *couldn't* be the meaning— could it? I decided to turn to John 17:3, which was one of the references listed in the margin:

> *And this is eternal life: it means to know, to perceive, recognize, become acquainted with and understand you, the only true and real God, and likewise to know him, Jesus as the Christ, the anointed one, the Messiah, whom you have sent.*

I had read that verse before, but now my spirit began opening up to the truth.

"According to these passages," I reasoned, "if I am in doubt about Jesus, then I cannot be certain about Jehovah either. To know one is to know the other!"

Of course, I knew a few *facts* about God: Jehovah is His name, He is the Creator, all wise, loving and powerful. But that was about all I knew. I knew facts—but *not Him.*

Pressing the issue further, I turned to 1 John 5:12 and read still another verse that had perplexed me:

He that has the Son has life; and he that doesn't have the Son of God doesn't have life.

"How can we have the Son?" I wondered.
And verse 20:

. . . and we know that the Son of God has come, and has given us an understanding, in order that we might know Him who is true; and we are in Him who is true, in His Son Jesus Christ. This is the true God and eternal life.

Then I turned back to 1 John 1:3, where John said that "eternal life *which was with the Father* was manifested unto us." And John said he had "seen him, touched him, *the Word of Life*" (1 John 1:1).

It bothered me that John consistently equated Jesus with eternal life. That seemed to say a lot more about Jesus than *I* had been taught! And I knew that the mere act of *suspecting* that Jesus might be more than just a created angel is about the greatest heresy imaginable to the Society—but logically, I could see no other conclusion. Mentally I listed the facts as they came to light:

73

1. Eternal life is knowing both Jesus and God.
2. That life is IN the Son.
3. Unless one has the Son he doesn't have eternal life.
4. That life, which was with God, was manifested unto men.
5. Jesus is the true God and eternal life!

Wow!

Had it not been for the gentle, unrelenting love of God, I suppose I'd have quit then and there. This whole idea was so foreign to my most cherished beliefs that I wanted to push it out of my mind—but it refused to leave. I began to see that the only way I could know God was through the Son; and that having eternal life was personally possessing the Son. My heart pounded as I struggled to open my mind to new truth. Through all those years of frustration, the real Truth had been standing beside me, offering Himself to me, but I'd been looking for a doctrine, a philosophy, rather than the Person Himself. There was only one honest course I could take: admit I'd been wrong and ask God to forgive me.

My lips moved silently as I prayed, "Jesus, You *are* my Lord. I don't understand it all yet, but I want my life to be open to You. I want You to come in and take control. Do what You will, but please forgive me for being stubborn—and so wrong. I was sincere, Lord—but that isn't good enough, is it? Forgive my sins. I've been trying to earn my way into Your favor and it hasn't worked. I know now that You didn't die just for Adam's sins, but for mine also. Possess my life. And just as

I was a slave of the Society, now let me be Your slave!"

There weren't any ringing bells, flashing lights, or heavenly technicolor visions; but there *was* an instant clearing away of horrible condemnation, and the deep inner peace of knowing that I now possessed Jesus and eternal life. Somehow I knew that from this moment I'd have a new relationship with Jehovah God.

Bowing my whole being before Jesus, I worshiped Him for the first time in my life, even as Thomas worshiped Him when he discovered He wasn't really dead but alive!

"Jesus," I said, "You're mine and I'm Yours."

And He answered, "Yes, I'm yours—forever!"

It had not been more than a half hour since Dan had left me alone in his living room. I could hear him in the kitchen talking with Gladys.

"Dan! That's it! My problem's solved. I've discovered Him!" I announced breathlessly, bounding toward the kitchen.

He smiled broadly, while Glad looked pleased. He had been explaining my problem to her.

"I don't know why I didn't see it before," I said. "The Society robbed me of something precious. Jesus is eternal life. God is eternal life. To have Jesus I must have God and to have God I must have Jesus. To possess eternal life I must possess Jesus, but that life *is* Jesus!" The words came as rapidly as I could say them.

"Hey! Slow down!" Dan ordered, laughing.

Turning to Glad, I plunged on without heeding him. "We've been robbed, Glad! They said no one could know Jesus like this any more. Tonight I met

75

Jesus and He spoke to me. He told me He would stay with me forever. I'm no longer a slave to the Society. If there are only 144,000 going to heaven, I'm *one* of them!

"Honey, I'm so happy for you!" she said. Less than two weeks later she had *her* name added to that heavenly roster. Our struggle for salvation was over. A greater miracle than our daughter's healing had taken place.

CHAPTER NINE

SPIRITUAL MISFITS

The days that followed were sweet but confusing. It was a relief to know that I didn't have to prove my worthiness any longer. Once Jehovah stood aloof and awesome, while I tried to chalk up enough merits to counterbalance His terrible judgments at Armageddon. But now I had real peace. If I wanted to preach door to door, I could—not because it was demanded of me, but because I sincerely wanted to. I had more joy than I knew what to do with!

But no religious experience can be maintained at peak intensity forever. The time soon arrived for reflection and evaluation of my new experience in the light of what I believed as Bible doctrine. As I quickly discovered, my new relationship with Jesus far exceeded my knowledge—and that bothered me!

By now the Society had completely forsaken us. Fortunately God's grace spared me any bitterness, even though we were rejected and made the objects of much gossip. But what a strange position to be in! We were unable to deny our Christ, but also unable to fit into the conventional church. For though our views about Jesus and miracles had changed appreciably, we still found it hard to break away from other J. W. viewpoints.

Much of my problem stemmed from being incapable of accepting, without question, the teachings of the historic churches. I didn't want to be identified with them. Their many doctrinal differences confused and annoyed me. "How can they be of God when they're so disgracefully divided?" I asked myself.

Some time later, a former J. W. wrote me from California telling me that she had accepted Jesus as her Lord after reading my testimony in a magazine. Her letter illustrates the problem I was having:

Dear Mr. Trombley:

What do I do now?

I started attending the ——— Church for a while to get adjusted. Everything is so different. As Witnesses, we were so active; but the apathy of these Christians appalls me.

So I started my personal witnessing program and praying for the sick. Somehow word got back to the pastor, who called me into his office and read me out but good. He forbade me ever to pray for the sick again unless he was present. That was *his* job, he said. Would you believe he told me to forget I was ever a J. W. and start acting like a normal Christian? He wanted to know why I couldn't be content to attend church and fit into their program. *His* problem is he doesn't have any program that is Bible-oriented.

I want to be obedient, but what shall I do?

Furthermore, I find it difficult to accept all their doctrines. The pastor isn't able to satisfactorily explain what he means by the Trinity, hell, etc.

Please don't tell me to find another church. They're all alike—unscriptural and dead.

Please write!

In Jehovah's love,
Mrs. S. T.

I wrote her a long letter, explaining that I understood her problem but I couldn't give her an answer. She really needed a half-way house where she could re-study her Bible under the guidance of the Spirit of God. Her real problem was the spiritual limbo she was in. She wasn't totally free from the Watchtower movement and its thinking; instead she was in a state of limbo, neither in nor out. Just like Glad and I were.

Merely leaving the movement and attending a historical Christian church doesn't free anyone from Watchtower thinking and practices. Long-established thought patterns must be reexamined. It's a whole new ball game; and what converted J.W.'s see in the churches sometimes hinders rather than helps them. Instead of getting firmly grounded in a Bible-based fellowship, they drift into one of the sixteen or more offshoot groups that have formed around the teachings of Pastor Russell—or they may start their own sect.

So Mrs. S. T.'s problem was witnessing. Mine was Jesus!

Now that I had made Him Lord, where did that place Him in the Godhead? Was He "eternally begotten," as the churches taught? How *could* He be eternal and still be "begotten"? And what about the Trinity? Did God have three different-sized heads on one body, or were there really three Gods, each with varying degrees of authority? The possibility was mind-blowing.

Still, I knew Jesus was my Lord!

The only explanation that seemed logical to my brainwashed mind was that of the Jehovah's Witnesses: There was one eternal God, Jehovah, who created Jesus as a "lesser god," whom He called Michael. At best then, Jesus was a "mighty god," but never the Almighty God! He must have had a beginning because the Scriptures say, "This day have I begotten thee" (Psalm 2:7). Before the day he was begotten, therefore, He did not exist! And the One preceding Him—the One Who brought Him forth—must be the true God.

YET I HAD MADE JESUS MY LORD!

Could I have two Lords?

If that sounds confusing (and it's the same problem that confronted Saul of Tarsus, a first-century "Jehovah's Witness"), how about this? Exactly Who or What was this Holy Spirit I had been hearing so much about? In the Pentecostal Church, everyone talked to Him/It as though He/It were a real person! I wasn't like the J. W. who, when asked if he had ever felt the Holy Spirit, replied dogmatically, "No, and I don't want to either." I had, and I did! But if any one thing came close to shattering my bottle of new wine and joy, it was these perplexing doctrines.

In the hope of finding solid answers to my questions, I ordered some literature from a Christian bookstore. When the postman delivered it, I attempted to force-feed myself, but it was no use. The book, *Systematic Theology*, by Berkof (a theologian of the Christian Reformed Church) ended the section on God with a muddled excuse that the Trinity was a mystery and inexplainable. That much I already knew!

Glad and I spent numberless hours hassling over one point after another, always ending right where we began: confused. Though I knew Jesus, I was still hypercritical in my thinking and saw everything through Watchtower-colored glasses. Unconsciously, I gradually slipped into the same position of most other deposed Russellites: that of naturalism. The Bible says, "The natural man receiveth not the things of the Spirit of God . . . because they are spiritually discerned" (I Corinthians 2:14). My appreciation for logical facts was keeping me entirely in the natural realm and unable to see through the eyes of faith.

The Trinity a mystery? Yes! And who wants to worship a mystery? How can you become acquainted with a mystery? I already had a satisfactory *explanation* of God, but that wasn't enough. I wanted to know Him *intimately*, like Abraham, Moses, and Elijah did. I didn't want a monologue with Him; I wanted dialogue.

So where did the Trinity fit in? I reasoned that the Trinity was probably the result of the early apostate church's attempt to clothe the eternal God of Israel in human flesh. I wanted nothing to do with such nonsense. I already knew what I believed, so I'd stick with that. At least I could explain "Jehovah God" from Scripture. Looking back now, I can see clearly the state of mind I was in.

I believe it was the hell question that ultimately pushed me over the edge. To a J. W., hell is nothing more than a weapon of the clergy, frightening

81

ignorant people into submission. I visualized a pond of liquid fire where God supposedly impounded countless humans and tortured them, burned them, blistered them, baked them, fried them, and damned them, but never let them get done. The God *I* served was a God of love and He was good. Besides, it's a lot more comfortable to see hell as the grave. After all, we all die eventually, and if hell is merely the grave, there's nothing to fear.

A decision had to be made. Glad and I prayed and asked for guidance and direction. But our resistance to historic Christendom made it almost impossible for us to get any clear guidance. We were spiritual misfits. We ended up agreeing that Russell had missed it on healing and Rutherford had missed it in a few other places—but the basic doctrines were correct, weren't they? "Why throw the baby out with the bathwater?" we asked ourselves.

We knew that Russell and Rutherford were guilty of false prophecies—but, on the other hand, it was impossible for us to accept the teachings of Christendom. Our decision seemed final! We would retain everything we had learned as Jehovah's Witnesses, except where we had discovered additional light. Consequently, there wasn't anything left for us except to go out and do our own thing.

CHAPTER TEN

DOING MY OWN THING

"Glad, I'm home!" I shouted as I ran into the house. "I've rented the Grange Hall and it'll only cost us ten dollars a night and we can use it every Thursday. I stopped by the paper office and put an ad in the *Times*." I paused to catch my breath. "Oh, yes, I had that new printer by Capron's Barber Shop make up some posters. How about that?" I asked excitedly.

"Terrific! When do we begin?" she asked.

"This week, if the posters are done. By the way, I didn't know what to call this thing. It isn't anything like the churches of Christendom, so we'll have to stay clear of any connection with them. But we can't call ourselves Watchtower Bible Students either. We've gone beyond them."

"So what *did* you decide on?"

"Oh, something real simple: *Crusade for Christ!* Sound okay?"

"Well, if that's what's on the posters, that'll have to be it, won't it?" she laughed.

"You'll have to play the piano," I said matter-of-factly, as I walked out to the kitchen and sat down at our round table with its yellow-and-green top. "It's a clunker, but it sounds in tune."

Glad set the coffee before me and then sat down

herself. She fully shared my excitement over our new venture.

"If it's half as much fun as the services we had in Sleepy Hollow, it'll be great!" Glad said, reminiscing about the first attempt we'd made to do our own thing just a few months before.

"Oh, *that!*" I replied. "That *was* fun, wasn't it?" I recalled how we had gotten permission to use an abandoned one-room schoolhouse and how we had announced on the local radio station that Oral Roberts, *via tape,* would be there.

"Remember how stunned you were when those three people came forward for salvation?" Glad teased.

"How could I ever forget that?" I laughed. "Who would ever have thought that a *recorded sermon* would produce results like that? You know, I didn't have the faintest idea what to do with those people!"

"I know you didn't. If Oral Roberts hadn't come to your rescue with instructions on the tape, you'd be standing there yet!" We laughed until the tears ran down our cheeks.

"The worst part," I continued, "was when we'd used up all the tapes a few weeks later, and the people asked *me* to preach!"

"I remember how nervous you were," Glad snickered.

"Well, after all, preaching a sermon is a lot different from making those little prepared talks I used to give over at Kingdom Hall.

"I know," Glad said, getting more serious. "But God helped you, that's the important thing. The people were blessed by your preaching."

84

"And now we're ready to launch into the next phase of this venture," I smiled broadly in anticipation. "The Grange Hall is much larger, and should be sufficient for our needs for some time."

"It will be exciting to see what happens," Glad replied with obvious enthusiasm.

During the days that followed, Glad spent considerable time on the phone calling anyone she thought might be interested in our attempt to convert the town to Jesus. She got very few responses—but as J.W.'s, we were accustomed to being persistent.

On Saturday, Gladys and I went to inspect the Grange Hall—an ancient, gray building that stood like a mute monument to apathy. At one time it had housed the Methodist Church, but that had long since been disbanded for lack of members and interest.

The ground floor, once used for classrooms, was now cluttered with rickety chairs, tables, dirty kitchen utensils, and what seemed like inches of dust. To the left and right were stairs that led to the sanctuary on the second floor. After trudging up two flights of creaking stairs in near-darkness, we were almost startled by the scarlet light filtering into the sanctuary through a huge stained glass window. The entire window was a magnificent work of art, picturing Jesus as the Good Shepherd, standing with beckoning hands and cradling a lamb in his left arm.

The pews, except for a few along the outside walls, had long since been removed, to make room for the Saturday night square dancers, who "squared their corners" under the watchful eyes of Jesus.

At the far end of the hall was a platform large enough to seat a hundred people; on the right end was the scarred piano Glad would use.

I was sure our first service in this ancient sanctuary would be as fresh and new as the now-budding leaves on the trees. Spring is my favorite time of year and the pure joy of seeing new life unfolding all around me only increased my sense of expectation as I nailed the posters to every available elm or maple tree.

On the Thursday evening of our first services, however, I felt a little uneasy. Glad and I had pulled six dark brown pews into the middle of the huge hall and arranged the lectern in the middle of the high platform. At seven o'clock—the announced time of the meeting—the pews were still empty. By seven-thirty, however, somewhere between twenty-five and thirty people were present— not a large number, but we thought it was a "nice group" to begin with. Still, they *did* look out of place in a hall that could easily seat 400. We recognized all of them: Glad's family, some Adventist friends, and Marie with her family. While Glad and I stood discussing how the meeting should be conducted, she noticed two strangers coming in.

"There are two people I don't know," she said, glancing toward the back of the building. A man and his wife were just entering the sanctuary. Walking over, we introduced ourselves, explaining that this was our first meeting and that we hoped they would enjoy the service and come back.

"I'm Norma Anderson," the woman said bluntly. "We're Pentecostal. This is my husband, Carl." They stood there uncertainly. "My husband's got Parkinson's disease. Know what that is?

86

It's the palsy." Her eyes began to fill with tears. "The doctors say he can't live more'n six months. Will you pray for him?"

As she wiped away the tears with the back of her hand, I glanced at her husband. He seemed all right at first, but then I noticed he was drooling a little at one side of his mouth. Not wanting to embarrass him, I reached out to shake his hand, and then I felt the steady, strong tremor.

"Certainly, I'll pray for him," I responded.

I knew nothing about his disease, but I knew Jesus was able to do anything. She said he had palsy, and Jesus had healed many who were "sick of the palsy." Was this any different? It was past time to begin the service, but I couldn't resist sharing with Mr. and Mrs. Anderson about Darlene's miracle. She said she had already heard about it and that was why they had come.

We started the service, but nothing went right! There were too few people; the room was too large and too empty; the ceiling was too high, and everything seemed strained and lifeless. We tried to sing a few familiar hymns, but the acoustics of the building conspired against us. The people moved their mouths but very little sound came out. From where I stood on the platform, I could hardly hear a thing.

Getting desperate, I swung my arms wider, higher, and lower—but still no improvement.

I tried harder by singing louder. But that didn't help; in fact, it made it worse. The next hymn was "What a Friend We Have in Jesus"—and as I announced it, I thought to myself, "Lord, if you don't do something quick and *be* a friend, I'm in real trouble!"

After that hymn, I decided to give up on the singing and start preaching.

On the lectern before me were two typewritten sheets filled with notes. "Surely there's enough material here to keep a person talking for more than half an hour," I'd said to myself after hours of preparation.

And I tried—oh, *how* I tried—to make that "masterpiece" last at least a half-hour. But in less than twenty minutes, I'd said everything I had to say. Here I was attempting to "feed the sheep" when I didn't have anything to give them. Frustrated and embarrassed, I resorted to the only thing left: prayer for Carl Anderson.

Trying to look calm and confident, I closed my Bible and said, "If there is anyone who wishes prayer for healing, would you please come forward!" I motioned for Mr. Anderson to come.

Grasping both sides of the chair, he struggled to his feet and started toward the front with slow, uncertain steps, sliding one foot ahead of the other. Keeping my eyes fixed on him, I left the platform and met him when he arrived at the front pew. Reaching out and taking both of his shaking hands in mine, I told the interested congregation about his problem and his request for prayer.

"We're going to follow the Bible instructions outlined in James 5:14 and 15, and anoint him with oil as we pray. He has said he knows God will heal him, and I believe He will too. Kneel down right here, Mr. Anderson."

After helping him get into a kneeling position, I placed my hands on his head and prayed, "Lord, this man says he believes You. Therefore, I ask You, according to Your word, to heal him."

Pouring some oil into the palm of my hand, I rubbed it on his forehead. "Mr. Anderson, you've been healed, according to the Lord's Word, from the crown of your head to the soles of your feet! Now go and be well in our Lord Jesus' name!"

He strained as he rose to his feet, and walked back to his seat just as unsteadily as when he came forward. Then I "heard" the silent accusations of the people who, moments before, were singing without being heard. Every eye was alternately fastened on him, then on me, and I could see the same question written on every face: "How can you tell this man he's healed when he isn't? Can't you see he's still ill?"

And then I heard another voice begin to mock me: "Hah! You've made a fool of yourself this time. You were so dead sure he would be healed—but he isn't! *Now* look what you've done! That man isn't healed. He still has palsy. What will you do now?"

I knew the congregation expected an explanation. Turning to them, I held up my open Bible. "According to this, Mr. Anderson is already healed. I've only done what the Bible said to do. The responsibility belongs to God. No human being can heal; that is God's work! But this one thing we can all be sure of—He will not fail to make good His Word. He only wants thankful obedience from us!"

Then I hurriedly dismissed the service with prayer. "This has to be the worst meeting anyone ever attended," I thought. I couldn't understand it. I had believed and prayed like Oral Roberts did on tape. Why did nothing happen?

Carl and his wife were the last to leave the sanctuary. As I shook Carl's hand, I noticed the disappointment on his face.

"Do you feel bold?" I asked him.

"Not exactly. Why?"

"Because I think you should go and tell someone that God has already healed you. It sounds crazy and it won't be easy, unless you like being laughed at. But you must hold fast to your confession and belief. How about it?"

He studied me for a moment while the idea sunk in. "Nah. How can I say I'm healed when I'm not? If I was healed, I wouldn't be shaking."

I paused for a moment, searching for just the right words. "It works like this for me," I explained. "Whenever I find myself beginning to doubt, I quote aloud the Bible verse dealing with that problem. You could quote a verse like 'I am the Lord that healeth thee' *—and then begin praising God for what you believe He has done for you; you'll soon discover that your thoughts are lining up with what you are saying. More than that, your body will start responding. Try it!" I urged.

"I . . . I don't know." He hesitated, then turned stiffly and started shuffling away.

"Wait just a second, will you?" I *couldn't* let him leave defeated. The whole service that night had been a colossal flop; *something* good had to come out of it!

"Try this, Carl! Start thinking something. . . ."

"Okay, but what?"

"*Anything*. Try counting one through ten—but not aloud, okay? Doing that?"

* Exodus 15:26.

"Yep."

"Now," I said, "start quoting the twenty-third Psalm aloud, but keep counting one through ten in your mind."

"At the same time?"

"Yes, keep them both going at once."

He started to laugh. "What are you laughing for?" I asked. "It's impossible, isn't it?"

"It sure is!" he replied.

"All right, the same principle applies to your sickness. Hebrews 3:1 says that Jesus is the high priest of our profession; that means He'll bring to pass anything you say if it agrees with His Word. When your mind wants to dwell on your shaking, begin quoting scriptures. You can't dwell on God's Word and on your symptoms at the same time. If you really believe, His Word takes over and your thoughts have to come into subjection to the Word. Got that?"

"I guess so. I'll try it anyway."

"Keep in touch and let me know how you're doing!" I called after him. "You're healed, you know!"

Though I really believed what I said, I doubt if anyone was much more surprised than I when Carl testified at the next service that all his shaking had stopped.

But the next few Thursday meetings were almost repeats of the first fiasco. The singing was as unenthusiastic as the singing down at the Kingdom Hall, and my sermons turned out to be rehashes of my Russellite doctrines. Still, the people stuck by us, and actually believed a good deal of what I was preaching. A good many of the people—like Glad's

91

family—were former J. W.'s who thought my ideas made a lot of sense.

Even though the services were pure drudgery, both Glad and I felt sure that better things were ahead.

CHAPTER ELEVEN

"CHUCK, YOU'RE DRUNK!"

The latter part of June is an exhilarating time in Vermont. Evenings are fresh with the fragrance of flowers and growing things. School is out for the summer, and kids' voices can be heard everywhere. On the last Thursday in June, Glad and I opened up the Grange Hall as usual, arranged the pews, and then went into a small side room to pray. Our hearts ached for something supernatural to happen.

"Lord," I prayed, "for Thy glory, do something!"

We knew something was missing—but what? After our prayer together, Glad left me alone and went out to wait for the first arrivals—but she soon returned.

"Chuck!" she said, her voice low but urgent, "Mike is here, and he's drunk. He acts like he wants to argue."

I rose immediately and started out the door. Glad was right behind me.

"Now listen!" she said. "You'll have to do something with him. What if strangers come in and see him like this? What will they think? We've tried so hard to make this work go!"

Her concern was understandable. This was our home town. Talk had gotten around that I had been "dismissed" from the Watchtower Society for getting involved with a Southern religion that believed in faith-healing.

When I found Mike, he was leaning against the door near the stairway. He was a likable guy, well over six feet tall, with dark hair and a disarming smile—but he had a serious drinking problem. We had worked together and had spent many serious hours discussing the Bible. In his early thirties, he already had two broken marriages behind him, but he said he'd found help from one of the Sabbatarian groups. We disagreed on many points but remained good friends.

"Hi, Mike! Am I glad to see you here!" Putting my arm around his waist, I started walking toward the empty pews. "Come in and sit down! We'll be starting soon."

Jerking away from me, he said with a a thick tongue, "Listen, old buddy! You're not doin' right! If you'd move this meetin' to Friday or Saturday and keep the Sabbath, *then* you'd be doin' right!"

"Let's keep our voices down, shall we?" I begged. "You're a good friend and I enjoy discussing the Bible with you, but this is no place to discuss the Sabbath. Let's shelve it for now, okay?"

"No, sir, Chuck!" He pushed me away with his arm. "You can't go on preachin' false doctrine to these people. You've gotta let me tell them the *real* truth!"

"Tell you what, then. Let's go pray first!"

Taking his hand in mine, I led the way, half pulling him downstairs to the unused kitchen. He was too drunk to resist. We couldn't find any light in the kitchen, but we did find an old chair. Both of us knelt by it in the dim light that shone in from the adjoining room.

I personally knew that Mike had a real hunger for God, but his compulsive drinking was his master. Reaching over to him, I put my right arm across his shoulders and rested my left hand gently on his forehead.

"God! Do something for Mike! Sober him up and deliver him from drink. Don't let the devil keep him bound like this any longer. He loves you and wants to do right, but he can't! He can't help himself. Please set him free! In Jesus' name!"

At first Mike was motionless; but then his whole body started shaking. In a moment, he jumped to his feet. Startled by his reaction, I also jumped up.

"What's wrong? Are you all right?" I demanded.

"I don't know, Chuck," he muttered, "but *something's* happened, that's for sure! I came in here drunk and now I'm sober. Hear that, Chuck? I'm *sober!*"

"Praise the Lord!" I shouted. Grabbing his hands in mine, I lifted them above our heads. "Jesus answered our prayer! You're a free man, Mike—*completely* free! Praise the Lord!"

But then something happened to *me*. My muscles became weaker and weaker, and I just gracefully melted to the floor. First, my knees buckled slowly. Then the upper part of my body seemed to collapse. The next thing I knew, I was in a pile on the floor, helpless to move.

"This is amazing!" I thought. "Mike came in

95

drunk and God sobered him, but I came in sober and now *I* feel drunk!"

Mike stood over me, trying to help me up. "Is there something wrong?" he asked anxiously. "Are you okay?"

I tried to answer Mike but couldn't! Something was taking place inside me, but I didn't know what. Unexpressed joy built up within me until I felt like a balloon filled with too much air.

"Chuck, will you answer me?" Mike demanded. "Are you sick?"

"Mike. . . ." That was far as I got in English. From within, there flowed forth a stream of words and phrases that were completely foreign to my ears. Like tons of water imprisoned behind a dam, thirteen years of desperation and hungering for God broke forth in a torrent of unintelligible words. On and on the flood continued. I was speaking in new tongues. Jesus had baptized me in the Holy Spirit.

The noise I created while exchanging my spirit of heaviness for the garment of praise reverberated from the kitchen into the upstairs meeting hall. Glad knew I had taken Mike downstairs for prayer; and when she heard this racket, she was both fearful and bewildered.

She rushed to the top of the stairs, and I can still hear her crying, "What on earth has *happened* to you?" It was several minutes before I could stop speaking in this new language and answer her in English.

We finally started the service, though somewhat late. During the singing, Glad played the piano while I helped out with my steel guitar; but because the afterglow of the Spirit was still bathing me in pure delight, my timing was all off.

"Chuck," Glad whispered, leaning over to me, "you act drunk!"

"Honey, I *feel* drunk," I replied, grinning apologetically. I felt as though I could play the strings off that guitar. Never had I experienced such exuberance and joy.

And then I noticed the congregation. They didn't know what had happened to me, but they surmised *something* had happened! I wasn't acting like myself!

We survived a rather "jumpy" song service; but when it came time to preach, the Spirit took control again. I stepped behind the little lectern and opened the Bible to my text; but before I could read a word I felt the same welling up within. This time, however, my nose had a funny feeling as though it were twitching, and my lips felt strangely tight. Then they started speaking—in English, but not what I had planned to say. My notes were in front of me, outlined in detail—but what I was saying wasn't written. Something new was happening!

It seemed as though scales were falling from my eyes, and the Lord was letting me see from one edge of eternity to the other, if that is possible. Between that span of time, *His* "Divine Plan of the Ages" was unveiled. (The basic foundation of Watchtowerism is the book, *The Divine Plan of the Ages*, in which a minutely-timed chronology is presented. Because this perverted system of Bible understanding was so thoroughly and deeply ingrained in my thinking, the Lord began here with His reconstruction.)

While the "new wine" overflowed, I found myself repeating exactly what I saw in the Spirit. The more I told, the clearer the vision became.

I saw—and what I saw, I said—and what I said, I suddenly believed!

As this was happening, I realized that God wasn't bringing me without my wife. Glad told me that when she heard me speaking, she *also* believed. Both of us had previously abandoned the idea of ever comprehending the historic teachings of the Christian church. But suddenly everything became clear! The fog moved out! It took the infilling of the Spirit to purge our spirits and our minds.

For the first time in my life, I began preaching Jesus as Lord. My congregation sat speechless and expressionless, except for their pursed lips that spelled another rejection. But by this time I was so filled with "holy boldness" that their hostility didn't seem to matter.

What I said under the anointing of the Spirit that night acted as a catalyst that caused some of our own family to reject us. "You've chosen your way," they told us later; "so you go your way and we'll go ours. Just leave us alone!"

It didn't take me long to learn that you can't force any spiritual experience down someone else's throat. The heartbreak of the months and years that followed that memorable evening is still a painful memory. When you're rejected by your family—well, that's a lonely experience.

But through my baptism in the Spirit, I had been clothed with a heretofore unknown power. The Holy Spirit made it clear that the baptism wasn't given to me merely that I might rejoice in a new-found freedom, but was given that I might witness for Jesus with the same effectiveness and authority that the early believers had after Pentecost.

Again I prayed, "Why me, Lord?"

And promptly He had an answer for me: "My Spirit will make all things real to you and you will take this message everywhere, beginning with this area and in your own home. Those who are against you now will also believe in due time. Don't be afraid; this is My ministry!"

CHAPTER TWELVE

BUILDING—THE HARD WAY

Three weeks after my baptism in the Spirit, we changed the meeting place from the Grange Hall to the Woman's Club right in the middle of town, and began holding services on Saturday evenings and Sunday mornings. Talk soon spread that a new religion was in town.

"And do you know who's responsible for it?" some were whispering. "That Trombley fellow. You know who *he* is . . . the J. W. who got mixed up in that Southern religion."

But the people came—some out of genuine interest, some out of curiosity. Parking was nonexistent. Those who attended our meetings had to make their way down an alley between a bank building and the theater, then down two flights of stairs and into a dimly lighted hall with dull yellow walls. We had decided to have the main service on Saturday night, when local folk who "went to town" might wander in.

Some did—and one Saturday night, shortly after we began the services, two retired schoolteachers cautiously entered and sat in the back row near the door. Both were well known, having held state honors as excellent teachers. If they intended to sit unnoticed, they failed. Every eye in the hall turned and watched them. Both Gladys Hyzer and Roxie Stokes loved God and were keenly interested in knowing Him better; however, this opportunity was denied them in the liberal church they attended.

Their reactions were amusing. Like most New Englanders, and especially Vermonters, they were not accustomed to outward expressions of emotion. The song service produced a mixture of gasps, startled amazement, and fearful interest.

When the meeting ended, they bolted immediately for the door. Less than five minutes later, they returned sheepishly. Gladys Hyzer handed me a song book.

"I'm terribly sorry," she stammered. "I didn't mean to take this book with me."

"What did you think of the service?" I asked her as I held my hand out for the book.

"Well . . ." she said, carefully choosing her words, "it's different from the Methodist church." Turning, she darted out the door a second time.

It was several weeks before they returned.

In the middle of the service, Gladys Hyzer raised her hand and asked if she could say something. I tried to conceal my surprise and beckoned her to stand. She rose, looking timid and unsure of herself.

"I'm not used to speaking in such a manner, so I ask you to forgive me if it sounds wrong," she said. "But I feel I should share my observations with you."

She nervously turned her head from left to right and then continued. "A few weeks ago my cousin and I visited you folks, inquiring about your manner of worship, and left here feeling that you were the *craziest* people we had ever observed. But somehow I've felt drawn back. And as I've sat through the song service tonight I've changed my mind just a little, and I am wondering if perhaps you're not the *sanest* crazy people I've met."

Chuckles and laughs could be heard everywhere.

"I've sat here and prayed," she continued, "asking God what this is all about. Your method of praise and worship is indeed strange to me. But then God showed me that your upraised hands and blended voices are like a heavenly symphony to Him. And now I'm convinced you're the *sanest* people I've met and I want to be a part of you if you'll allow."

We did, she did, and finally she was baptized in the Holy Spirit.

Every service was filled with the power of the Spirit. As word got around, people began driving long distances to attend the meetings. Gradually, even my family began to respond. And when my mother, who was a very proper lady with a Welsh background, received the Holy Spirit in one of our evening services, I thought I had seen the greatest miracle of all!

It wasn't long before several of the believers in the fellowship expressed the conviction that we should have our own building. My immediate reaction was negative. The year before Darlene's miracle, the Kingdom Hall had been built with donated labor and "squeezed" finances, and neither came easily. Everyone had been happy and proud when the building was dedicated for the "glory of Jehovah and His service," but the many struggles involved were still too fresh in my memory.

But that wasn't the only reason for my negativism. Most of those favoring the building idea were women—which was all right—although I wondered why the men weren't showing more interest. Besides, we had only $200 in the bank. Yet, the reasoning of the women sounded very logical, I had to admit.

"The uncertainty of meeting in a rented hall isn't good for the children," one of them said.

Another asked, "Have *you* ever tried to teach children in a kitchen?"

Finally I agreed to bring the matter before the fellowship. We certainly needed the room and the security a permanent building would give.

After several seemingly fruitless prayer meetings, we were still uncertain how to begin—or *whether* to begin. No one had received any positive guidance. But finally, when we were ready to abandon the whole notion, God impressed me with an idea about buying a certain piece of land. Excitedly I told the rest of the fellowship about it.

"You've missed it," several of the men chided. "No one would build *there!*"

The land was a corner lot just outside the Bellows Falls city limits, in a little village called Gageville—total population, 400. It was a narrow strip of land wedged in between a steep hill and the main road. For a building as large as a church to be constructed there, the lower part of the hill would have to be removed. After taking a second look at the lot, I began to doubt the source of my revelation.

"And what will we do for money?" another man asked sarcastically. That was a subject I didn't really want to face. Because of my strong Watchtower background, offerings and financial drives

103

nauseated me. "The clergy of Christendom are antichrists because they constantly appeal for money," we had argued.

But another obstacle loomed even larger than money. The men in the fellowship were all dubious about the venture—so who would help me with the building? I knew very little about construction and the one man who could advise and guide us wasn't enthusiastic. Yet in my heart I knew the Lord had said to purchase that piece of land.

Intellectually, it seemed absurd to consider the idea any further—but if this was what God wanted, who was I to argue? So with the words of my brethren burning my ears, and the devil's whispers of discouragement in my soul, I decided to lay out a "fleece." If the land wasn't for sale, I'd apologize to the fellowship and confess that I'd been mistaken about my guidance.

Early Monday morning, just as the sun crested the tops of the trees and started warming the crisp fall air, I began my detective game of tracking down the owner of the land. I began by quizzing the neighbors in several directions around the lot, asking two questions: "Do you know who owns the land on the corner?" and "What would you think if a little church was built over there that might increase the value of your property?" No one knew who owned the land and no one objected to having their property values raised.

Finally I visited the Beebee Plumbing Shop, housed in an old red barn within a stone's throw of the corner lot. "Do you know who owns that piece of land?" I asked the office girl.

"Why, Mr. Beebee does," she informed me.

"Then he's the man I must talk to. Is he here?"

104

"He's in the back shop. I'll take you to him." She led me into the back room, where Mr. Beebee was brazing some antique copper pans.

"Mr. Beebee?" I inquired. "I'm Charles Trombley, and I must buy the piece of land on the corner. This may sound strange and even way out," I apologized, "but Jesus my Lord has directed me to buy it and build a church there."

I waited. Mr. Beebee was a big man, and a lighted cigarette was hanging loosely from his lips. He cocked his head to one side as if to let the smoke escape without burning his eye.

"You want to build a *what* there? That piece of land isn't good for anything. Did you say you wanted to build a church there? Where would you get your water? And what about sewerage? There isn't any city water or sewerage out this far yet and won't be for some years. The Bellows Falls line is just about 800 feet that-a-way," he pointed with his brazing torch. "You gotta be crazy."

"Well," I countered, "I haven't had time to consider *those* things—yet. All I want to know is, will you sell that piece of land, and for how much? You said it isn't any good, so apparently it's a liability to you, but the Lord told me to buy it."

He pushed himself lazily off the bench and stood upright. Sticking his thumbs in his belt, he hitched up his pants. "You're flat serious about this, ain't you?" he muttered. "Well, I'll be *d—ed!* I don't think it'll work, but if you want that land, I'll take your money. Tell you what. You can have that piece for $175, and I'll furnish the water and sewerage. You can hook into the big house. Won't cost you but twelve dollars a year. How does that grab ya?"

105

"I'll take it!" I nearly shouted. "Will you do whatever paper work is necessary? I'll get the money for you!"

Thanking him again, I left with every fiber of my being shouting the praises of God. That night I told the fellowship how Jesus had worked out the details and the almost ridiculous price Mr. Beebee asked. Some rejoiced, while others still seemed skeptical. But our treasurer gladly wrote out a check for the land, leaving us twenty-five dollars in the bank. This was October, and winter would soon be upon us. It wasn't exactly the best time of year to be thinking of building.

Two weeks later, Harold Stevens unloaded his green-and-yellow John Deere crawler tractor at the site and began removing the lower part of the hill and digging the foundation. The tractor was a small one with a four-foot blade, which he used in his logging operations. The job took many hours, but since Harold was donating the work no one complained.

November came. The weather was turning cold, but there had been no hard freezes. As the first loads of sand, gravel, cement and blocks arrived, the bank account again showed exactly $200. We had discussed several methods of financing, but most of them frightened us. We prayed again. Jesus again assured us that this was His work and that He'd provide the funds as we needed them. So we all agreed that we'd build with what was freely given, without any pressure or appeals whatsoever. If Jesus didn't provide on certain weeks, then we wouldn't work.

Saturday was "work day" but in the beginning

only one elderly man showed up. He had only one good hand, since his left fingers had been amputated because of cancer.

"Where are the other men?" my lone helper asked me.

"It's like this, Mr. Snide. They're not sure this will work, so they're staying on the side lines. You and I are the two nuts—so welcome to the camp!"

After a while, I imagine he too was beginning to suspect my sanity. He had to tell me how to mix the cement, and the first row of cement blocks I laid looked like the work of a drunk—as Mr. Snide laughingly pointed out. He had suggested that we use a line level, and neither of us had taken into consideration that a long line stretches. Therefore the blocks were high on each end and low in the middle.

Our big break came when a minister from a neighboring town heard what we were trying to do and, being a bricklayer, volunteered to lay up the starter corners.

As November wore on, the days grew shorter and darkness settled in around 4:00 p.m. I went home only after it was too dark to see any longer. By the time I got home, I was dog-tired. Long-unused muscles told me I was crazy, and my skinned knuckles burned as I scrubbed the grime from them. On Sunday I scrubbed especially hard, and even raided Glad's bleach bottle in an effort to whiten my grubby hands; but nothing really worked so I'd apologize to the church because their "preacher" was working for them.

By the time December came, the basement walls were nearly finished. The weather was still cold but not cold enough to freeze the ground. Mr. Snide, my helper, suggested we buy some salt and add that to the cement.

"It'll keep it from freezin'," he said.

It seemed to work, but later I discovered it made the joints flake and much of it had to be dug out and replaced. Money came in just fast enough to keep us busy, but without any surplus.

By January, the walls were finished; and amazingly they looked straight! Snow covered the ground, but the temperatures hadn't been low enough to cause a deep freeze. With some extra money, a commercial bulldozer was hired to "backfill" around the walls.

A typical Vermont freeze set in by mid-January, pushing the temperature to 45 degrees below zero. The soft backfill, mixed with snow, froze into a solid, expanding mass. A few days later, I was shocked to see that all four walls had been pushed inward as much as three feet. I sat on a snow bank and cried like a child. Weeks of hard work seemed to be ruined. Large cracks had appeared everywhere along the walls.

The next day I stopped at a local lumber yard and asked for advice. They sold me several two-by-twelve-inch planks and, following their instructions, Glad and I began chipping away at the now-solid backfill. I'm sure the neighbors were snickering at what was rapidly becoming a comedy; but God intervened again. Several of the brothers came to our rescue and, using house jacks and planks for reinforcements along the entire length of the walls, we gently forced them back into place. Fortunately, the footing didn't split. Then we set about digging the loose mortar from the cracks and refilling them with fresh cement.

By the middle of March we were nailing the floorboards down. That too must have been a strange sight. For every man, there were two women—some using two hands on the hammer and missing many of their "hits."

On some days the floor looked like a squirrels' convention at a nut factory. People were everywhere, giving an occasional howl of pain as they missed a nail and smashed a finger—but it was fun. Lunchtime was like a large picnic.

During April and May, the sidewalls went up and amateurs rapidly became semi-professionals. Instead of my smashing a finger daily, now it was every other day. Once, while driving a sixteen penny spike into a staging brace, I hit it harder than usual, missed the spike completely, and squarely struck my thumb. For the next few minutes I danced a jig, holding my smashed left thumb in my right hand and saying "Praise the Lord" over and over.

June—time to raise the rafters, but how? Bob, my brother, was the high-school custodian. He talked with Cliff, the manual arts teacher and challenged him to come up with a design that would leave the inner part of the building free from supports. This is easy with steel—but we were using heavy, green, native lumber.

Not only did Cliff's design work; it also had some local builders "eyeballing" it and taking notes.

Jesus was still guiding every step. Our financial load increased considerably, but so did the income and the volunteers. Jesus was providing, exactly as He had said He would.

109

We decided to do a little prefabricating, first laying out the heavy spruce rafters on the ground and then assembling them into huge, triangular frames. Imagine, if you will, a group of men hoisting these frames onto the ten-foot sidewalls. First one corner was lifted to the top of the sidewall, then the other—leaving the huge inverted V with its peak resting on the floor. We then nailed several two-by-fours together for a "pusher" and used this to ease the peak to an upright position. After much struggling and straining to get the first two frames into place, we were ready to start raising the rest of them.

Because of the space required to swing the frames into position, it was necessary to slide each erected frame the entire length of the building and lean it against the first two. After getting all the frames hoisted and stacked at the end of the building, we began sliding them into their proper positions.

In order to keep the frames from falling, we tied a rope to the apex of each one before moving it. One man volunteered to sit up on the peak of the first two frames and hold the rope.

"Hold it tight, now," I told him. "Wrap it around your hand and hold on. Above all, don't let go! If that frame falls, it will end up in the basement. Got it?"

He nodded with a grin, while two other men tied long ropes to the corners of the frame and began to pull, sliding it precariously along the top of the sidewalls. Two more fellows helped by walking behind the frame, kicking it along. Long lines of cars stopped and watched, and we heard some people say it would be the miracle of the twentieth century if someone didn't get killed. But we laughed and praised the Lord as each frame went into place.

When we were sliding our sixth or seventh frame into place, I heard a cry from above:

"I can't hold it! I'm losing it! Look out! There it goes!"

I looked up at the man holding the rope and jumped back instinctively. Helplessly, I watched as Walt Welch jumped aside, grabbed a window frame and swung out of the way just as the frame passed him like the jaws of a huge pair of shears.

With a crash it hit the first floor and, without hesitating, it went right through into the cellar.

"Well, hallelujah anyway!" I heard someone shout.

Looking back now, I realize why the Lord permitted us to be a public spectacle. Other evangelical groups had tried to invade this conservative section but none of them had aroused any interest. But *everybody* was interested in our "crazy building program," and we made many friends in the process.

By July, the damaged floor had been repaired, and the roof was nearly completed. The weather was extremely hot and humid. Stripped to our waists, we men turned as dark as Indians, as we laid row after row of asphalt shingles. Several days were so hot that the shingles actually pulled apart if we stepped on them.

In August the yellow birch flooring was nailed in place. A plywood factory in northern Vermont gave us enough paneling at cost to cover the interior walls. The heating plant was supplied at much below cost by a local Catholic dealer. Another

Catholic furnished all the lighting at cost and installed it free.

As the time for the dedication drew near, the work days were at times twenty hours long. Exactly fourteen months had passed since Jesus became Lord and Master of my life. Not having quite enough money to finish the project and not receiving any stop order from the Lord, I approached one of the local bankers. After I had told him what we needed and said that I was unable to give any denominational guarantees and had no financial backers, he said he'd let me know. Less than a week passed before he called me into his office.

"Mr. Trombley, this is highly irregular, but I've talked with the board and they've agreed to let you have the money. However, we're not going to secure it with a mortgage in the name of the church —not yet anyway. Would you be willing to give me a gentlemen's handshake—just between you and me—that you'll personally see that the payments are made on time? Your record is gold-plate, so we'd prefer your word on this."

"But, Mr. Allen, isn't it necessary for something to be contracted? I've never received money on a handshake before."

Taking my hand in his, he gripped it firmly. "I believe in you and what you're doing. Come back in a year, and if the church is able to make the payments by that time we'll draw up a mortgage. Does that sound all right?" he asked.

"All right? It's absolutely perfect!"

At last the building was finished and the dedication service—attended by several local ministers— was over. Although our congregation wasn't very

112

big, it was the largest charismatic congregation in the state and the first in that area.

That evening, after the quiet of home engulfed us again, I wondered how far this would go and what the future held for us. I hadn't wanted to get this deeply involved. It frightened me to have people calling me "Reverend"—a truly dirty word to J. W.'s. But more frightening than this title was the responsibility Jesus had given me for leading the sheep, feeding them, and seeing that they grew spiritually.

CHAPTER THIRTEEN

THE LORD PROVIDES—ALL KINDS OF THINGS

Shortly after the new building was dedicated and named "The Tabernacle," the congregation agreed that I should quit my secular job and give my full time to the ministry.

"It'll give you more time to win souls, and the work will grow faster," they argued. "And you'll grow spiritually with more time to pray and study." I had many misgivings about the idea; but after much prayer and much debate, both with the Lord and with the members, Jesus gave me peace and assurance that He would be my sole source. All I had to do was please Him in all things. His promise was, "If you'll take care of My affairs, I'll take care of yours."

On the surface, the situation appeared utterly impossible. After the utilities and other normal operating expenses were deducted from the current income, the fellowship came up with a "fair" salary of twenty-five dollars weekly. That was it. There were no other benefits. Actually it was far less than we needed, even though we owned our home free and clear. Had it not been for Glady's happy attitude that "the Lord will provide," I might have balked even more than I did.

Furthermore the Society had continually hammered into our thinking the idea that all clergymen of Christendom who "work" for salaries are antichrists. Freely we had received, so freely we were to give. It wasn't easy to give up this kind of thinking. Jesus had to reassure me several times that "the labourer is worthy of his hire" (Luke 10:7).

Finally, I agreed to the twenty-five dollar weekly salary and gave my notice where I worked. When I got home that night, I added up our weekly expenses for gas, auto payment, groceries and other necessary household items—and for the umpteenth time I reached the conclusion that there just wasn't any way I could stretch twenty-five dollars *that* far. But I'd committed myself to the Lord and the fellowship, so I couldn't turn back now. Still staring at the page of figures, I called for Glad to come into the office.

"We've really blown it this time," I informed her with a note of defeated sarcasm. Look at these figures again! There isn't *any* way we can get by on twenty-five dollars, regardless of *how* honorable our motives are. Figures are still figures and bills are still bills, and no way do they balance."

The more I talked, the more upset I became. Nervously, I drummed my fingers on the edge of the desk while Glad stood by my side studying the figures, exactly as she had done several times in the past few days. Looking up, I noticed a silly grin on her face.

"Now that we're in this mess, what do *you* propose we do?" I asked impatiently.

Seating herself in the hardback chair near the desk, she reached out for my hand and held it to her face.

"Chuck, we've been over all this before. Didn't

115

Jesus say He'd provide? He provided for the church building, and He's taken care of us so far. I can't understand how you can be so fearful before anything has happened."

Her response was gentle and I knew she understood how I felt, but still it stung me. "That's because you don't pay the bills," I snapped defensively.

Pulling my hand away from her, I rose from the desk and started to leave the room, still deeply troubled in my spirit.

"Chuck," she called after me, *The Lord will provide!* You wait and see!"

"Grr . . ." I thought to myself. "That's easy for *her* to say. What would a woman know about such things?"

Alone in the bedroom, I poured out my heart to the Lord and asked His forgiveness for my lack of trust. I knew that doubting His Word was the same as calling Him a liar, but I couldn't shake those negative feelings. Gradually He restored my calm and gave me the reassurance that Glad was right, even though I couldn't see *how* He would provide. It was only a matter of days before Jesus began showing me how.

It happened as a result of the first missionary service our fellowship had. Glad somehow got separated from me and ended up sitting on the opposite side of the church. The missionary from Borneo related his adventures and finished his message with a financial appeal. This type of service was completely foreign to me (Jehovah's Witnesses don't have traveling missionaries as such and never take offerings for them), so I'd granted him permission to do whatever he was accustomed to.

In his appeal he told us how badly he needed a boat for his work. It sounded like a good project, and I wanted to help him out.

In my wallet was exactly one dollar, but I knew that Glad also had a dollar with her.

"I'll give mine," I assured myself. "She still has hers to buy gas for the rest of the week."

When the offering plate was passed, I dropped my dollar in without a moment's hesitation. Even though I was now badly "bent," I wasn't completely broke; Glad still had her dollar. I felt good; I had a dollar invested in that boat.

Sitting in the car after the service, I remembered the dollar and turned to Glad. "Honey, I put my last dollar in the offering tonight."

She dropped her head back against the seat and laughed infectiously.

"What's so funny?"

"Please don't get upset," she replied between chuckles, "but I knew you had a dollar so I put mine in the offering, thinking you'd surely keep yours. Wow! We'll *really* have to trust Jesus now, won't we?"

"That was a stupid thing to do," I chided. "Look at that gas gauge; there isn't enough gas to get us home."

Provoked, not that I had given my last dollar but that *she* had, I wondered what to do next. When the gas gauge in that Buick said empty, it meant it—and it had been registering empty all the way to church. Pulling out of the church parking lot, I started off in the opposite direction from home.

Still a little annoyed, I looked straight ahead and

117

said nothing for a moment, although I had figured out a solution to the problem. One of the men in the fellowship worked at a Texaco station at the bottom of what we called "Red-light Hill." I'd go there and ask him for a dollar's worth of gas until I had the money. Finally, I answered Glad's question.

"There's not enough gas to get home," I said. "I'll have to ask Lloyd to give us some on credit till I can get the money to him. I hate the thought of asking him—but what else can I do?"

Just as we reached the top of Red-light Hill, the Buick slurped the last drop of gas. Slipping the transmission into neutral, I coasted down the hill, timing it so that we made it through the green light at the bottom. Our momentum carried us across the little square, and the car stopped directly beside Lloyd's gas pump.

Lloyd shuffled out in his usual quiet way and, without saying a word, started pumping fuel. The figures on the pump quickly passed the one dollar mark.

"Hey! That's enough!" I ordered.

"Aw, this here's on me tonight," he mumbled. I blinked my eyes and wondered if I were hearing things.

Leaning against the trunk of the car, I watched silently until he finished. Pulling some paper towels from the rack on the side of the pump, he began cleaning the windows.

"Lloyd, there's something I must confess," I began hesitantly. "Both Glad and I unknowingly put our last dollar in the offering tonight. I was going to ask you for credit on the gas, but—thanks loads!"

" 'Tain't nuthin' " he replied unemotionally. "Before I left church tonight, I felt the Lord nudge me to give you some gas." He continued cleaning the windows without even glancing in my direction —but I detected a somewhat sheepish grin on his face.

As we drove home, my heart bubbled with joy, realizing that Jesus was concerned over such seemingly small matters. Glad broke the silence.

"The Lord provided, didn't He?"

"He sure did!" I admitted, a little ashamed of my lack of faith.

I had learned, though, that God often allows us to be pressed by needs right up until the very last minute.

I remember the Saturday we were out of groceries. I was down at the new building, working on the lawn and wondering how God was going to supply our needs. About that time, my brother Bob stopped by.

Sticking his head around the corner of the building where I was raking grass seed into the soil, he said matter-of-factly, "I put two bags of groceries on the back seat of your car. And, oh yes— there's an envelope with some 'lettuce' for a new suit." He turned and started to leave.

"Hey! Wait a second! Who sent it?"

"The Lord sent it!"

"And what did the Lord look like?" I questioned.

"Preacher," he said laughingly, "that ain't none of your business."

Not all of the Lord's lessons on commitment and trust were that positive, however; some seemed negative—like the burning of the farm, for instance.

Fall with its beautiful blaze of warm colors had turned into a white wonderland. More than three feet of snow was on the ground, and ice was six inches thick on the pond.

Around 2:30 one morning, I was startled awake by the urgent blowing of a car horn. Jumping out of bed, I ran to the front door and snapped on the outside lights. The road out front was slippery and narrow, and piled high on both sides with big banks of plowed-out snow. I could just faintly make out Don McClain's car stuck in a snow bank. Don was a Christian boy who had been boarding at the nearby farm where Glad's parents used to live.

"What's the trouble?" I yelled, as I flung open the front door.

"The farm's burning!" he yelled frantically. "Better come quick!" I looked in the direction of the farm; and sure enough the sky was brilliant, lighting the whole countryside with eerie red and orange shadows.

Quickly, I ran back into the house to rouse Glad. "Glad! Get up now! The farm's on fire!" I said, shaking her to consciousness.

Glad could hardly believe what I was saying, but when she pulled back the curtains and glanced out our bedroom window, she understood the urgency of the situation.

While we dressed quickly, we heard the local fire trucks stopping out front. When I looked out again, I saw they couldn't get through because Don's car was stuck crossways on the road! Don was spinning his wheels furiously, trying to get out of the snowbank, but it was no good. Firemen were pushing and shoving on the car and arguing about what should be done.

"Look at that, Glad," I yelled. "The place will burn to the ground before they get there!"

Finally the men succeeded in jamming the car even further into the snowbank, leaving just enough room for the trucks to pass. Precious minutes had been lost!

Glad and I ran to the farm just behind the trucks. When we arrived, Glad's brothers were throwing everything they could out the windows, while the volunteer firemen struggled with hoses and cursed about the distance to the water supply —which was at least a quarter-mile away through waist-deep snow.

The main house on the farm was connected to the ancient barn by two garages and workshops. It made one long unit, typical of many early Vermont farms. When we arrived, the fire was well into the main house, which Papa Allen had built during the depression. He had refused all outside or welfare help, saying, "Jehovah will take care of His own." For building material, he used whatever was available—second-hand lumber, with shavings and sawdust for insulation. Long dried out, it literally roared into flame.

I held Glad's hand as we stood there staring in disbelief. In the front living room was a small old-fashioned crib, made of iron. It was cherry-red from the heat.

"It's hard to believe, isn't it, Glad?" I asked.

Holding onto my arm, she started singing, "Jesus Is the Sweetest Name I Know."

"What're you singing *that* for?" I asked.

"Do you realize that I'm losing years of savings? All my antiques and cut glass are gone. The keepsakes for our home. The things the boys sent me

121

from overseas. It's all gone! All those things I had saved in the little room over the kitchen—they're all gone!" She paused momentarily. "And, honey, Jesus has given me the sweetest peace about it all. I should be nervous, crying and upset, but I'm not. This is my birthplace. All my memories from childhood are in this old house. I . . . I . . . don't understand it, but He's given me an unexplainable peace."

After the fire was out and only the pungent smell remained, we dug through the piles of rubbish and sooty scraps, searching for anything salvageable—but found nothing. Everything that had belonged to Glad was completely destroyed. Her cut-glass collection was a solid mass. Even the dishes left in the kitchen sink had melted into a mass.

Later that afternoon we notified the insurance agent about the fire and our loss. He called back an hour later and informed us that someone had made a mistake. When they insured our new house, our belongings in the "little room" at the farm had been left out. He was sorry, he said, but there was no coverage and nothing he could do.

Again Glad sang, "Jesus Is the Sweetest Name I Know," and still her inner peace remained. I knew it had to be the Lord, although I didn't quite understand what He was doing.

"Glady," I said, "we never had peace like this when we were Witnesses, did we?"

She was so choked up she couldn't answer.

CHAPTER FOURTEEN

DOXOLOGY IN TWO FLATS

Over the New Year holiday, Zion Bible Institute in Providence, R.I., was to hold its annual convention. Since Dan Cornelius (my spiritual "father" in the Lord) was a Zion graduate, he suggested that we all go.

Sitting at the desk in our living room the night before the trip, I figured our expenses almost to the penny, and found we had something like four dollars left over for unexpected emergencies. But Jesus had told us to cast all our cares on Him—so I was sure we had nothing to worry about.

Glad packed a large lunch before we went to bed, and the next morning she filled two large thermos bottles with hot coffee. Before we left the house, we held hands and asked our Lord to give us a safe and fruitful trip without any accidents or mechanical failures.

The ninety-mile trip to Providence was uneventful, and we arrived at the huge red brick auditorium in time for the morning service. For some two hours we sat spellbound, not only by the tremendous singing but also by the "messages in tongues." At lunchtime, we picked our way through the throng of people to the cold car parked directly in front of the auditorium. As I was unlocking the door, I heard Glad groan.

"What's wrong?" I asked.

"There's a flat tire!" she wailed, pointing her gloved finger at the left rear tire. "Didn't we ask the Lord to give us an uneventful trip?"

"But the *trip* was uneventful," I replied. "It's a good thing we didn't have this flat on the way up here." I walked around to the driver's side and unlocked the door. After opening the trunk I handed the keys to Glad.

"Better start it up and get the heater warm. It's bitter cold out here."

About that time, Dan ambled up casually. "Troubles, eh?" he said, walking back to the open trunk. "Got a spare? I'll help you change tires."

"But *that,* dear friend, is the problem," I said helplessly. "I don't *have* a spare."

"Interesting, interesting!" Dan grinned. "What're you going to do *now?*"

Looking around, I noticed a garage across the wide boulevard. "There's a filling station over there," I said. "I'll take the tire over and have it fixed."

"No wonder that tire's flat!" Dan remarked. "The fabric's showing through so badly, I doubt if it can *be* fixed. Didn't you know how worn that tire was when you left?"

"Really, Dan, I hadn't paid that much attention to it; but I've *got* to get it fixed. I only have four dollars so I can't buy a new tire."

While I jacked the car up, Dan walked slowly around the car, checking the other tires. "You aren't going to like this, Chuck," he said upon returning to my side, "but you've got another flat on the front."

"Don't even joke like that!" I ordered.

Dan threw back his head and laughed. "Hallelujah anyhow!" he sang out. "It'll work out; it always does!"

At that moment, my sense of humor was missing and I honestly couldn't see anything funny. Glad got out of the car to see what the laughing was about, but quickly noticed my dejected face.

"*Now* what's wrong?"

"Take a look at the front tire. It's flat too!"

We stood there staring at each other blankly. Finally Glad said, "What do you suppose He's trying to show us now?"

"I don't know," I sighed. "All I know is we've got two flat tires, no spare and only four dollars in cash."

"Oh, well," she said, responding to Dan's humor, "He's provided all along so He'll provide now, won't He?"

She returned to the warmth of the car while I removed the back tire. As soon as I had it off, I saw it was beyond repair. The inner belt was fully exposed in places, and the sharp edges of the ice had pierced both the liner and the tube. Then I examined the front tire and saw the same problem there.

"You know, Dan," I said, "I'm glad I had a tube put in this tire the last time it was flat or it wouldn't have lasted this long."

"I'm glad to hear you saying that," Dan replied. "There's always something to be thankful about, isn't there? The Bible says we're to give thanks in everything—so praise the Lord anyhow!"

"Praise the Lord even when you've got two flat tires?" I thought. "This sounds a little ridiculous. . . ." I stood there staring at the sidewalk for a moment. "Okay, Dan," I spoke up at length, "let's walk over to that station and see what kind of deal they'll give me."

After I told the youthful attendant my problems, he went to the back of the station and pawed through a pile of old tires. He finally came up with one that he said I could have for three dollars, though he claimed it was worth much more. I took it, and had one dollar left.

"Got any suggestions about the other tire?" I asked Dan.

"How about using a truck liner?" He explained that it would reinforce the fabric and just *might* get us home. After more searching through the junk bin, the attendant found one and I paid my last dollar for it.

When we finally arrived back at the car, Glad was anxiously waiting. I reported our situation and then told her, "We'll have to pray this buggy home in faith. The weather report says it's going below zero tonight, and I don't relish the thought of any more flats out in the middle of nowhere."

"That would be terrible. . . ." Glad murmured, her voice trailing off as she visualized us stranded along the road on a sub-zero night.

"But praise the Lord, Glad!" I spoke up, trying to bolster my own faith as well as hers. "We're His responsibility, aren't we?"

"Yes, that's true," she replied, "but I was just wondering about our own inconsistency in asking God to take care of us and then bringing along an emergency fund—*just in case He didn't make good*

126

His Word. Isn't that the same as mistrusting Him? If He said He'd be our source for everything, why did we need an emergency fund in the first place? Doesn't that nullify the promise He made to us?"

"I hadn't thought of it in that light," I replied, "but it does make sense."

Up until that time, I hadn't yet discovered the real strength inherent in true praise. But now I was beginning to see. All I had to do was give thanks in all things and be obedient to God. Jesus hadn't promised to change our circumstances, but He *had* promised to supply real peace and joy. I discovered the act of praise actually releases God's power into our circumstances, to change either them or us according to His overall design.

Seeing this, I turned over to Him our seemingly impossible situation; and although we were still a long way from home and had two bad tires on the car, we praised Him.

Before the afternoon service began at 2:30, both tires had been successfully rigged; we'd finished our cold lunch with hot coffee; and after spending some time worshiping the Lord, we were ready for the service.

The rapture of singing with 2500 people and the unexcelled preaching of Dr. L. Heroo made the rigged tires belong to another world and time— that is, until 10:30 that night when we started for home.

"I'll follow closely in case you need me," Dan offered.

"Let's all pray before we start," I suggested. Joining hands, we stood on the sidewalk and thanked the Lord, according to Mark 11:24, for a safe journey home. I reminded the Lord that we were there to worship and adore Him, and asked Him respectfully to provide some new tires for the car.

It must have been as miserable a trip for Dan and those in the car with him, as it was for Glad and me. I didn't dare drive over twenty-five or thirty miles per hour, for fear the tires would be punctured by the sharp edges of the ice and packed snow. Nearly every bump convinced Glad that one of the tires was going flat. The tension for the first hour was tremendous, and our conversation was limited to an occasional "Praise the Lord!" We were *trying* to trust Him, but it wasn't easy.

"So far, so good," I'd frequently say under my breath to reassure myself and ease the tension.

The ninety miles stretched into what seemed like a trip around the world. When we finally arrived home at 3:00 a.m., bone-tired from tension alone, we just sat in the car for a few minutes with bowed heads, thanking Jesus for His faithfulness.

"Let's go in and get to bed; I'm beat," I said. Picking up an armful of picnic leftovers, I headed through the dark for the front door, only to stumble over something on the cement steps.

"Did you leave anything on the steps?" I asked Glad. "I nearly fell!"

Stepping over whatever was blocking my entrance, I flicked on the light. Both Glad and I saw them at the same time.

"Praise the Lord!" we shouted simultaneously, as we looked at two brand new winter tires. Picking one of them up, I turned it on end and noted the size.

"These'll fit the car, and they're the real thing— not retreads. Wonder who left them?"

"That doesn't really matter, does it?" Glad said. "The Lord provided, didn't He?"

Rolling the tires into the house, I said, "This sure beats the old J. W. days, doesn't it, Glad? Do you realize we hardly ever got an answer to prayer back then?"

"Well, we hardly ever prayed for anything," Glad reminded me, "so it's not surprising that we seldom received anything."

"But I wonder what they'd say if we told them about these tires? Surely this proves that God actually *does* pay attention to our prayers."

"But they've got an answer for everything, Chuck. They'd say it would have happened anyway, even without prayer."

"Yes, I guess so," I agreed. "Probably what it comes down to is this; some people believe what they want to believe, no matter what evidence they see to the contrary."

"It's sad, isn't it?" Glad said as she unbuttoned her coat. "They're so sincere but they just don't realize what they're missing."

It was three weeks later that I met Don McClain again. After the farm had burned, he had rented a room several miles away.

"Hey!" he called out to me. "Did you find those tires?"

"Were *you* the one who left them? That was one of the most exciting answers to prayer I've ever had! God really knows what we need, doesn't He?"

"I hope so," he replied dejectedly. "Boy, I don't know why the Lord's so good to you; He never does anythin' like that for me."

"What do you mean?" I replied, half puzzled and half amused.

"I worked hard to save that much money," Don wailed, "and then the Lord told me to give the tires to *you*. Boy! Sure wish somebody'd do somethin' like that for me."

"Don't you have any tires yet, Don?" I quizzed. I remembered the slick tires that blocked the firetrucks the night of the fire.

"Nah, not yet," he said.

"Then perhaps you'd better take these back," I suggested. "You need them as badly as I do, and I don't feel right about accepting them."

He stood upright from the slumped position he'd been standing in. Taking a deep breath as though to assume command, he looked directly into my eyes.

"Can't do *that*. Jesus told me to give them to *you*." Then he raised his voice almost angrily: "But I sure wish He'd do something like that for me!" He then went on to tell me about an experience he'd had the previous winter. He needed an overcoat, and had been asking the Lord to send him one. All winter he shivered, but still no coat came in. Being in Bible school, his funds were limited.

That spring, long after the need had passed, a Christian woman came to him and apologized. "Don, I'm sorry. The Lord impressed me to give you this top coat last fall, but I just kept putting it off. Forgive me, and please take it now."

"Lady, I don't need the coat no more," Don replied. "Boy, sure wish you'd obeyed Him last winter. I needed that coat then."

The experience had left him in a very grumpy

state of mind about the workings of prayer. And yet what beautiful obedience he had manifested in giving me two tires just because Jesus *told him!* His only problem was that he hadn't learned how to be joyful in obedience. I knew I had to teach him what I'd learned about praise.

"Listen, Don," I told him. "I want to share something with you. Instead of grumbling because you have to be obedient to God, why don't you start praising the Lord that you gave me the tires? Of course, I could give them back, but that wouldn't be obedience on your part. So just be grateful that He used *you.* If you praise Him, He'll take care of you. That's what I've found out. We're to give thanks in every situation in which we find ourselves."

"Well, it's easy for you to say that," he replied. "You're a preacher."

"But this is a principle for *all* Christians, Don. There's great power in praise, and God wants you to have this power. You see, praise is more than just worship; it's a means of spiritual combat. There will be times when you'll have to force yourself to do it—but do it anyway. As you praise God, you'll begin to see your circumstances changing."

He shifted his position and said, "Maybe so. I don't know."

Surely, I thought to myself, someone as obedient and sensitive to the Lord as he is shouldn't be *that* unhappy—so I continued.

"You'll have to admit, Don, that David had his share of trouble, right? And what was his attitude? In Psalm 34:1, he says, 'I will bless the Lord at all times: his praise shall continually be in my mouth.' You see, he wasn't using praise as a handle to get

131

something from God. He had simply *decided* to thank God in all situations. And that's what brings total release, Don. God wants you to praise Him no matter *what* happens."

He left, still mumbling. As I watched him slouch off, I thought to myself, "What a strange combination of obedience and grumbling!"

But then the Holy Spirit seemed to say to me, "Yes, I've noticed that about *you*, too. . . ."

CHAPTER FIFTEEN

WHO LOCKED THE DOOR?

There were thirty-five of us kneeling in our living room, praying together and enjoying God, when Sam burst into the room unannounced. He stumbled over feet and legs.

"Where's my wife?" he demanded angrily. "I've come to get my wife. She doesn't belong here with you nuts!"

He stood in the middle of the room, weaving from side to side. He was a short Jewish man, but seeing him from our knees made him look menacingly huge. His Gentile wife, Betty, looked at him with embarrassment written all over her ashen face. She had started to get up when he spotted her. Grabbing her arm, he dragged her out to the little Rambler parked in the drive.

For a moment I was too shocked to move. Then I said to the other men, "Let's go! He might hurt her!"

When Sam saw us running after him he started his bellowing again: "Don't you come near me," he threatened. "You've ruined my home!"

His face was flushed, his black eyes full of hate and anger. Still holding onto his wife's arm, he turned on me and shook his fist in my face. He was so close that I could smell the stale liquor on his breath. "You've messed up my home, you and your fool religion!" he snarled. "I'm going to sue you for everything you've got!"

"Everything I've got belongs to God, Sam!" I replied.

In all my days I'd never faced a situation quite like this. I prayed silently, "Lord, if you don't do something soon, I'm in real trouble."

Betty evidently realized that it was hopeless to reason with Sam when he was like this, but she tried.

"Sam, I . . ." she tried to explain.

"You shut your mouth, woman! If you'd stayed at home you wouldn't be in this trouble!"

Turning to me again, he started cursing. "See this roll of dimes? I'm going to knock the h— out of you!" He lunged toward me, the roll of coins clutched in his fist. Retreating a step, I braced myself, not knowing what to expect.

Just then Glad stepped to my side as bold as John the Baptist and said, "Sam! I rebuke you in Jesus' name!"

Her sudden appearance and her words startled me. "Glad! Go back in the house!" I whispered. "Don't you know you're not supposed to talk to a Jew like that?"

"What?" Sam snapped back. "What?"

"I rebuke you in Jesus' name!" Glad repeated.

Without saying a word, Sam turned, shoved his wife into the back seat of his car and slammed the door shut. Then he hopped into the front seat and started backing off.

We all stood silently watching until the dust from his spinning tires had settled; then we turned and went back into the house.

After discussing the circumstance, we thanked the Lord for His help and prayed for Betty and Sam. Inwardly, though, I was troubled with questions. Why had I just stood there when Sam lunged at me with that fist full of dimes? Why hadn't I fought back? Sam wasn't a large man, and since he was drunk, I should have been able to pulverize him. Ordinarily I *would* have. But something kept me from swinging my fists.

Suddenly I knew what that "something" was. Jesus! Had I given Sam a beating, I'd have brought terrible reproach on Him. But there He was, right when I needed Him—restraining me and taking all the "fight" out of me!

"Thank you, Jesus! Thanks for being so near." The old J. W. idea that God was far away seemed almost silly now. He was not only near—He was *in* me!

Still, though, I felt somewhat ashamed that it had to be Glad whose rebuke caused Sam (or the evil spirits in him) to leave. But it was a good lesson. I saw that evil spirits *do* submit to believers who use the name of Jesus in faith.

In a little while, the prayer group left. Glad and I assumed that everything was settled and that the unfortunate scene could be forgotten. Less than two hours later, however, the phone rang. Glad answered.

"Who?" she asked, not even getting a chance to say hello. I could hear rapid talking on the other end of the line. "What? But you can't. . . ."

When the other party hung up, she stood for a moment as though in a daze.

"What's the matter?" I asked. "Who was that?"

"It was Sam," she replied. "He said he's going to shoot you!" Her face drained of all color as she replaced the phone receiver.

"Oh, no!" I groaned deeply. "Why didn't he just go home and leave us alone? What else did he say?"

"He said he's coming right out, and that you'll meet your God tonight!"

"Glad, I don't know what to do," I said helplessly. "Maybe we ought to call the patrol—just in case. I don't want to do anything foolish that would ruin our testimony and destroy all we're trying to do for God, but I don't know what else to do."

"Well," Glad answered hesitantly, "he *is* drunk, and he might hurt someone, driving in that condition. Maybe the patrol ought to be called for that reason, if for no other."

When I talked with the patrol dispatcher, he said a trooper would be along shortly; but nearly half an hour passed before the green and white cruiser pulled into the drive. I hurried out to meet him, and we stood on the lawn and talked for a few minutes. After writing down the information I gave him, he started to leave.

"What're you going to do?" I asked him.

"He's probably trying to frighten you. If he does come back, call the dispatcher and I'll come right away. I'm on my way to Grafton but I'm in constant communication with the office." He returned to his car, and Glad and I watched him drive off.

"He's only going to Grafton," I said to Glad. "That's only twelve miles away. Wonder if he can beat Sam's bullet if he *does* decide to shoot at us?"

I joked. It was a terrible attempt at humor and Glad was not amused.

While she went into the house to put the children to bed, I stood gazing at the sky. The stars were out, and somewhere in a nearby tree a whippoorwill was singing its special song. Just being alone with God in His huge universe was reassuring. I returned to the house, confident that God would care for us.

"There's a car!" Glad exclaimed shortly after I closed the door.

Out of the shadowless night, two headlights shimmered into view and then turned into our drive. The engine stopped and the piercing headlights dimmed and died. For a moment all was silent. Then the sound of a door being slammed shattered the tense stillness. Pulling back the shade, I peered through the bedroom window.

"Turn out the lights!" I ordered. "Make sure the children are in the back bedroom. I'll see if I can talk to him."

I could barely make out the form of a staggering figure crossing the lawn in the dim light. He passed directly in front of the picture window, then disappeared from view. In a second, I heard him stumbling up the steps leading to the front door.

"Open this door!" he demanded as he angrily rattled the door knob. Then he threw his shoulder against the door. I wondered if it would hold.

"I'm gonna shoot you, preacher. Get ready to die!"

"Jesus, here we go again!" I prayed. "I don't understand what this is all about, but please take care of my family. Don't let them get hurt!"

Cautiously, I felt my way to the front door in the darkness of the room. "Why don't you go home, Sam? You're drunk."

My mouth was dry and had the taste of fear in it. I'd been in some tight places before, but I couldn't recall one as frightening as this.

"You'd better open this door before I break it down!" he shouted as he continued pounding and pushing.

But the door held fast.

Meanwhile Gladys knelt by the bedroom phone, calling the police. Thinking I might be able to draw his attention away from the house and the children, I slipped silently out the back door and slowly felt my way alongside the house. My mind refused to come up with any workable plan. What could I do? How was I going to distract him long enough to get the gun away from him? And could I hang onto him until the trooper arrived? No, that idea was out; the trooper wouldn't be here for half an hour.

In seconds, I reached the end of the house and peered cautiously around the corner. Not fifteen feet away, I could see Sam twisting the doorknob and cursing me for not letting him in.

"What if that door opens while I'm out here?" I didn't even want to think of the answer to that one. "Better get back inside!"

Silently retracing my steps the way I'd come, I heard Sam let out a curse. "D—— you, preacher, I'll get you yet!"

Back in the living room, I knelt in the doorway between the living room and the bedroom, where Glad was talking with the police. I was in a direct line between Sam and the children. "At least," I reasoned, "I'm between him and my family. Wish I could think of something else, though."

Then I remembered my hunting rifle in the bedroom closet. Going to the closet, I picked up the rifle and slipped a 30-30 cartridge into the chamber. Returning to my kneeling position in the doorway, I started shaking uncontrollably.

"What's wrong with me?" I thought. "There isn't anything to worry about. I'm a good shot, and this thing can blow both him and the door into kingdom come."

I eased the hammer back and hip-aimed the barrel at the center of the door. The shaking grew more violent.

Suddenly, I knew what was wrong. *Jesus* wouldn't fire that rifle—and Jesus was in *me!* "I can't!" I screamed within myself. "Jesus! Help me!" Tears welled up in my eyes as I emptied the chamber carefully and put the gun back in the closet.

Suddenly I was overwhelmed by His presence. He was *really there!* Contrary to what I'd been taught at Kingdom Hall, Jesus was there, keeping me from doing something that would have ruined my ministry forever.

Silently, I praised Him for saving me from making such a horrible mistake. Returning to my kneeling position in the doorway, I continued praising Him both in English and in tongues, softly but audibly. His presence brought a surge of strength.

Suddenly it was quiet! The struggle at the door ceased. "Why doesn't he do something?" I wondered.

Seconds seemed like hours. My palms were wet with sweat, my breathing rapid. Then Sam's harsh voice broke the silence again. He was now directly outside the bedroom window. The shades were drawn, but Glad had turned the bedroom lights back on to quiet the whimpering, frightened children.

"What're you doin' in there?" he growled. "Calling the police? Won't do no good. I'll get you sooner or later."

"Sam? Can't you hear the children crying? You're scaring them. Why don't you go home and act like a man?" Glad said.

"Home? Your fool husband ruined *my* home and I'm goin' to get him for it." His voice trailed off —and then silence again. But the relief was only momentary. Suddenly the whole area was bathed with the brightness of his automobile headlights.

"Do you suppose he's turned those lights on to see better?" Glad asked. "No! Listen! He's leaving! Praise the Lord! He's leaving!"

Glad comforted the children and assured them that their daddy wasn't going to be shot. Together we thanked God for His protection.

Then I checked the front door to see if Sam had damaged it. What I discovered shook me.

"Glad, did you lock this door before Sam came?"

"No, I left that to you. Why?"

"Because *I* didn't lock it!"

"What are you trying to say?" she said, gasping. "It isn't locked!"

We both froze. It was a long moment before the realization of what had happened penetrated our fear-paralyzed minds. But suddenly we both "thawed" at once.

"Do you realize—" I began—

"—that we've just witnessed a miracle?" Glad concluded.

We didn't know whether to laugh or cry. Trembling with relief, excitement, and joy, we hugged each other.

"Better call the Highway Patrol and cancel that call," I said to Glad. "Who needs the cops when God's got His foot against the door?"

Next morning, after some short and fitful periods of sleep, the phone rang again. I looked at my watch; it was exactly 9:00 a.m.

"Mr. Trombley? This is Lieutenant Smidley of the Highway Patrol. We picked up Sam Levine after your call last night."

"Where?"

"His car was parked along the highway in Gageville. We found him standing on the road, sick. We confiscated a loaded gun from his car. Will you come in this morning and file a complaint?"

There was a long silence while I pondered the "Jesus approach" to the matter. I didn't want Sam to get into any serious trouble. Glad and I had discussed it last night and agreed that the whole incident should be lesson enough for Sam, after he sobered up.

"I'd rather not, lieutenant. Can't you just warn him and let it go at that?"

"But what good will that do?" the lieutenant protested. "If you don't file a charge against him, our warnings will mean nothing."

"Well," I replied, "I'd still rather not press charges. Whatever you do is entirely dependent on whatever laws he's broken. By the way, where is he now?"

"We turned him over to the local police and they

kept him for a while last night, but then released him early this morning. They can't hold him without some complaint against him. That's up to you, Mr. Trombley."

"What about the gun?" I asked.

"He has a legal permit for that. He wasn't apprehended with the gun as he threatened you."

"Still, I'd rather not. . . ."

The officer broke in. "If that doesn't beat all! This guy threatens your life and the safety of your family and you let him off scot-free!" He sounded exasperated.

"Well, sir," I tried to explain, "it's because of Jesus. There was a time when I'd have had it out with him once and for all, but I have no desire for revenge now. All I want is for Sam to discover the same peace in Jesus that I've. . . ."

"Thank you. If you change your mind, call me!" He abruptly hung up.

"Glad, do you realize what's happened to me?" I said as I turned toward her. "This isn't like me. You know that! Just a few months ago I'd have insisted they give him the whole treatment; but honestly, I don't have any hatred for Sam at all. Wow! We're no longer J. W.'s, that's for sure! By the way, is there any coffee made yet?" Suddenly I was both hungry and feeling great.

Later that evening, as we were again recalling the events of the day before, I said to Glad, "You know, if I had just *known* that God had His great foot on that door, I would have acted a lot differently than I did. I just can't get over the fact that Sam couldn't open that door, even though it was unlocked. Of course, he was drunk—but not *that* drunk, because he was able to drive his car."

"Well," Glad said, "I guess we've both learned a new measure of trust in Jesus, haven't we?"

"We certainly have. I now see very clearly that the only way we can get to know the Lord intimately is to allow Him His choice in the problems He permits, as well as the solutions He sends. God's in control of everything, and all He wants us to do is trust Him."

"What a beautiful lesson!" Glad exclaimed.

"And one other thing, Glad. Next time there's any rebuking to do in Jesus' name, I'll do it!"

CHAPTER SIXTEEN

NOT BAD, FOR AN OLD LADY!

"Do you remember that woman from Grafton who used to work for the Salvation Army?" Glad asked while reading the morning mail.

"Alice Hough? What about her?" I asked.

"Here's a letter from her asking us to come and pray for her. She fell and broke her back, and it's so serious her doctor tells her she'll never walk again. She's seventy-two and all alone now. Sounds urgent. We'd better go out today, don't you think? This letter is dated three days ago."

We agreed that we'd drive to Grafton and visit Alice that afternoon. On the way out, Glad filled me in on forgotten details. Alice and John Hough, members of the Congregational Church in Grafton, had visited one of our joyful fellowship meetings on a Saturday night quite some time ago. That night, there had been a manifestation of worship in tongues, and I confess I was a little anxious about what their reaction would be.

But afterwards, when I asked Alice how she liked the service, she replied with a decided British accent, "It's different from the Congregational Church we attend in Grafton—but good—and it sounded genuine. A bit explosive, perhaps, but I like laughter. Jesus *is* alive, you know, so why should we have a gloomy religion?"

As Glad refreshed my memory, I began to look forward to visiting with this sweet old woman who now pleaded for our prayers so earnestly.

We found Alice flat on her back in a hospital bed in the living room of her home. Suspended over her head was a steel bar, which she apparently used to shift herself from one position to another.

"How did this happen?" Glad asked.

Motioning to an antique chair nearby, Alice said, "Pull up a chair, honey, so I can talk to you. Your husband can bring that chair from over there.

"John had a gallbladder attack—over there in the bathroom." She pointed toward the corner of the room, where there was an open doorway. "He called for me to help him. As I put his arm around my shoulder, he passed out. When he fell, he threw me off balance and I fell across the tub with him on top of me."

X-rays had revealed that the lower vertebrae were crushed and jammed together. At her age, the doctors didn't expect them to mend and, having done all they could, they sent her home.

"The best I can hope for is a wheelchair, they said." Her voice was suddenly quieter but more intense. "But I don't think that's Jesus' will, do you?"

Before I could answer, she reached for my hand and continued softly: "The doctors can't help me, but I know Jesus will heal me if you'll lay your hands on me." She took my hand and placed it on her forehead. "That's why I've asked you to come and see an old lady. You're the only people I've met around here who believe Jesus will heal anyone. Everyone else just feels sorry for me!"

My heart was thrilled at such simple faith. Oh,

that all His believers might accept His words with such confidence! "I give you praise, Jesus," I said almost inaudibly. "Thank you for this dear lady who doesn't doubt You or Your Word!"

Suddenly the room was literally flooded with His presence.

"Alice," I said, "the gracious presence of the Holy Spirit is here right now. I can't do anything for you—except pray and love you—but He's here and He'll make good His Word."

Tears were running down our cheeks; but they were not tears of sorrow. True compassion, generated by the power of God, was reaching out to release the affliction that had "crushed" this dear child of God. As I gently put my hand on her white hair, the Spirit bore witness with my spirit that she was being healed. When I finished praying, her eyes were fixed on me.

"I love God with every part of my being," she said, "and I know He has healed me just like He said He would!"

She was so childlike and trusting; but then, hadn't Jesus said it was this kind of faith that touched Him? Feeling inspired to encourage her, I asked, "Alice did Jesus *really* hear us and heal you while we prayed?"

"He certainly did!" she replied almost indignantly, yet smiling. "You don't doubt Him, do you?"

Leaning over, I raised her right hand to the lift above her head. "Now then, will you take hold of that rod and roll over on your side? You told me you couldn't do that—right?"

Without any hesitation she obeyed. Gripping the rod until her knuckles turned white, she turned her body over—her eyes never leaving mine. I saw the sparkle in them and smiled at her.

"Alice, I praise Jesus for you! He's healed your broken back! I really do have to run now, but when we come back to see you, I expect you to be up and able to serve us some cookies and tea. How about that?"

"Honey, I'll do that!" she said.

We left her lying on that bed; but we were fully assured that the Lord Jesus had visited that room in a special way. The pain, which is normal with a back injury such as hers, was completely gone.

In a few days we received another letter from her:

Dear Brother and Sister Trombley:

I just wanted you to know what happened. I had to go back to the hospital and couldn't understand why. But now I know.

The doctor took several more X-rays because I wasn't supposed to walk again; but he couldn't find anything wrong. The vertebrae are in their correct positions and those that were crushed are all healed.

The doctor doesn't understand it, and neither do I, except that Jesus is so lovely. I shared my testimony with the doctors and nurses there. Now I am home again, walking and able to do my housework. That's pretty good for an old lady of seventy-two, isn't it?

Thank you for your prayers and thank Jesus for His power.

> Sincerely in His love,
> Alice Hough

"Glad," I said, after reading the letter, "do you realize the depths of what has happened to us?

Why, only a few years ago, had that woman asked for our prayers, we'd have been powerless to help her."

"Yes, it would have been a story with a far different outcome," Glad agreed.

"You know what I would have told her, had she asked for my prayers when we were J.W.'s? I'd have said, 'I'm sorry, old lady, the day of miracles has passed!'"

Recently we visited with Alice Hough again when we were in Grafton for a series of Bible studies. We found her well and hearty, a healthy seventy-five years of age. During our visit with her, she told us about an occurrence that does more than verify her healing.

Her home is more than 100 years old, and the supports in the ancient cellar needed replacing. Carpenters, already overloaded with work, gave her no assurance that they could or would come. In her frustration, she left the matter with the Master Carpenter.

That night, she said, she had a dream in which she saw herself building the forms, laying the stones, mixing the cement—doing everything that needed to be done, even to using two stepladders and making beams from two-by-eights.

"Honey," she said to me, "I couldn't find anyone to help me, so Jesus reminded me that He had already shown me how to do it. He even showed me how to load the stones—I got them from that stone wall over there—into a wheelbarrow so an old lady could push it. Took me several months, but I did it. 'Course I couldn't use a shovel to mix the cement, so I used a big kitchen spoon. Three spoonfuls of sand to one of cement—that's the way He said to mix it, so I did. Can you imagine? Me, an old Britisher, becoming a carpenter at seventy-five? Come down to the cellar and I'll show you what Jesus and I did."

She took me to an old dirt cellar. In a narrow passageway barely three feet wide, I saw her handiwork: three cement posts about two-feet square and some six feet apart. It was a job that would have taken an experienced man two days to complete at the most; but she said it took her from November to May, working several hours a day.

"What an amazing person!" I told my wife later as we drove away. "She talks about Jesus as though He were living there with her. No wonder she has such great faith."

On the closing night of the Bible studies, she visited the service. As we ministered to the sick, I looked up and saw her standing there.

"Lay your finger on this little skin cancer," she said, grasping my hand and placing my finger on an ugly-looking scab on her nose near her left eye. "Just pray and it'll be all right."

Then God revealed to me something else she hadn't mentioned. "Is there something wrong with your heart?" I asked.

"You leave my heart alone!" she said, rebuking me with a wide smile. "That's my passport to Jesus. I'm eighty and all alone. I want to be with my Jesus—and if you pray for my heart, He'll heal me and I might have to stay here another ten years. See?"

"Can't do that, Alice," I replied. "I'm committed to the work of Jesus, who came to set the captives free. If Jesus wants to release you from your heart trouble, then we can't argue with Him, can we? So let's pray, and if He hears you, then accept it. He loves you, Alice, and whatever He does will be a manifestation of that love."

"Okay," she said with her heavy British accent, "go ahead and pray."

At last report, her heart is fine, the skin cancer is gone, and she's still walking with Jesus. That's not bad. for an old lady!

CHAPTER SEVENTEEN

HIS MYSTERIOUS WAYS

"I can't believe it!" the visitor in one of our Sunday services said to me. "*You* were a Jehovah's Witness?"

"That's right," I grinned. "The Lord's able to save *anybody!*"

"That's wonderful," our friend said, "but you'll have to hand it to the Witnesses on *one* thing."

"What's that?" I asked.

"Witnessing! Why, if we born-again Christians had half the gumption *they* have, we'd be winning converts by the thousands."

"Not again!" I groaned within myself. I'd heard that comment from born-again Christians until it had become obnoxious to me. So again I found myself explaining what I had explained dozens of times before: A. J. W. doesn't witness because he wants to necessarily, nor because he has a Life-giving message to share. Rather, he's trying to prove himself worthy of gaining life! In other words, it's the old heresy of salvation by works.

But do born-again Christians witness about Christ because they *must?* No! A thousand times, no! Christians witness because they *want to!*

But even that is not the whole story. For while

all Christians *desire* to witness for Jesus, not all are *able*. Some have not yet discovered the power of the Holy Spirit. Consequently, I was thrilled as one after another of my "flock" were baptized in the Holy Spirit and began to share the exciting reports of their attempts, successes, and failures. I praised the Lord with a joyful heart as I watched them grow in the Lord and reach out to others.

Some discovered Spirit-imparted abilities and talents they had not had before. One elderly teacher found herself composing and singing spiritual songs without premeditation—something contrary to her natural personality. Others, who were introverted "loners" discovered an awakening power within them that allowed them to feel at ease with others. The fear of man that snared them was gone!

Even in the little daily tasks, they found His presence available. One woman told me of a beautiful deliverance from depression. "I was ironing in the kitchen last Tuesday night," she said. "Vic was working and I was having a real battle with negative thoughts. For years the devil had been having a good time with me, and when I got like that I didn't have any ambition. I lost all interest in living. I'd been like that for years, and I was sick of it."

"So what did you do?" I inquired.

"Well, since I've been filled with the Spirit," she continued, "I've come to know that many of my problems are caused by Satan. I've also learned that Jesus has provided me with complete victory. So I set my iron down and deliberately walked to the door and opened it. 'Satan!' I ordered. 'Get out of my house and get out of my life and leave me alone—in Jesus' name!' Then I slammed the door and went back to my ironing. I've been free ever since, praise the Lord!"

"Did they ever return?" I asked. "Those little voices—the negative thoughts?"

"They did, but I've been doing like you said to do. I praise Jesus regardless and, as you said, the thoughts line up with the confession. By keeping my mouth filled with Jesus-talk, I haven't even given my thoughts an opportunity to play tricks on me. It's taken some time to re-educate myself, because I've been depressed so long—but hallelujah! I've got the victory now!"

How I rejoiced when I heard of this manifestation of the Holy Spirit's power!

And then there are Roland and Thelma Stevens. I'll never forget the first time they attended one of our fellowship meetings. Being members of the Church of the Nazarene, they came only to "straighten us out" and prove to us that tongues were "of the devil."

When Thelma was younger, she had polio. This had left her with crippled hands and ankles that were barely usable. Roland had had a serious alcohol problem that left him with ulcers and bad nerves.

As they returned to our services time after time, I watched their hostilities gradually melt away. Finally, the day came when they too were baptized in the Spirit and received healing for their afflictions. I marveled as I watched them become zealous witnesses for Christ.

One day Thelma and her friend Joyce Brown, shared a thrilling testimony with our fellowship. Both of them were new at witnessing, and they decided to begin by visiting the sick at the local hospital. When they came to one particular room, they were doubly excited with they discovered a Mrs. Blanchard, who was the daughter of an ardent Johovah's Witness. Having learned how to deal with Witnesses through our meetings, they let her to Christ and then asked permission to pray for her sickness. Mrs. Blanchard told them she was awaiting surgery for the amputation of both her legs. A serious diabetic condition had caused them to become gangrenous.

"We laid our hands on those almost-black legs," they said, "and asked Jesus to heal them—instantly! Next day when Dr. Hebb checked her just before surgery, he discovered a change in color; so they put off surgery for another day. By then the circulation was normal, and the diseased flesh healed—so she didn't have to lose her legs!"

It's needless to say we were all excited and thrilled, but I'll say it anyway: We were *thrilled!*

Since then, Roland and Thelma have founded the New England School of Theology and built a very successful church. They have a radio program with a healing ministry that's left a trail of miracles across New England.

Not all the experiences were this dramatic, but each was thrilling. One Sunday morning the teacher of our Junior boys failed to appear for the morning service. Because he usually led the singing, I delayed the start of the service for several minutes. Then in desperation, I went to his classroom to see what was wrong. There in the middle of the floor, surrounded by his energetic boys, he knelt praying with each one individually. The Spirit had fallen in a special way during the class, and all but one of the boys had accepted Jesus as his Savior.

When I explained the delay to the congregation, they began praising the Lord with such vigor that I never did get to preach that morning!

While some of our Spirit-filled members attended Bible schools and prepared for the ministry, others ministered with great power where they worked. When one young fellow purposed to follow the Lord, he fasted for thirty-five days to receive the baptism in the Spirit, but only got hungry and thin. He soon learned that the gift of God isn't *earned*, but received through simple faith. His main problem was his extremely introverted personality. After his encounter with the Spirit of Christ, nothing short of a miracle happened. He went back to his job and soon won six other people to Jesus!

The wife and children of the Jewish man who threatened my life were baptized in a river, and she was powerfully filled with the Spirit. Her uncertainty and timidity were soon overcome with the incoming of His power. Even her husband settled down and started giving more attention to his family.

Several Mennonites came who had been warned by their pastor not to attend. "That man is an antichrist," he had said. "There's so much happening down there, it *can't* be of the Lord!" But I guess his warnings only made certain people curious. They came, and many of them received the power of the Spirit!

In time, some of the women decided to form a Women's Mission Society. I was invited to attend one of their first meetings and in that meeting one of the women received a revelation about how to help feed the poor in the community.

"Let's plant a big garden, preserve the vegetables, and this winter we can distribute them. What do you think?"

Immediately, I too received a "revelation"—about who would end up doing much of the work!

"I pass," I said with a grin.

But they voted me down and went ahead with the project. It didn't take them long to borrow several acres for the summer—but as feared, we men found ourselves playing farmer. We plowed, "busted clods" until our hands were blistered, and bent over planting seeds until our backs wouldn't straighten. But when it was finally finished, we all felt good and watched with expectation as row upon row of green beans, potatoes, and corn pushed through the dark soil.

Because of Vermont's erratic growing season, garden crops are a gamble. You plant early and hope there isn't a late spring freeze; if there is, you must start all over again and then hope there won't be a summer drought.

It was nearing the last of May when the weather report said there would be a freeze that night.

"Chuck, help us!" Glad ordered, as she began calling members on the telephone.

"What're you going to do?"

"Cover everything with newspapers. We'll need all the help we can get!"

Two hours later the temperature was already falling rapidly. We worked feverishly, covering the young plants with newspapers anchored in place with loose dirt. Standing to ease my aching back, I looked over the all-too-many uncovered rows.

"This'll take till Jesus comes, and *then* it'll be too late." I remarked.

"Stop talking and get to work," someone shouted laughingly.

"No, I've got a better idea!" I replied. "We've prayed for just about everything imaginable; why not about a simple frost?" I called everyone to join hands and stand in a circle.

"Lord, this is your work," I prayed. "These gardens were planted to help the poor and the hungry. We're willing to do the work, but we can't control the weather—that's Your department. So we commit these fields to You and praise You ahead of time for keeping the frost off these plants!"

Without waiting for anyone to question me or make any remarks, I said, "Let's lift our hands and offer Him thanksgiving!" Afterward, we all glanced out over the rows and rows of vegetables that were yet uncovered, and then headed for home—sure that somehow it would be all right.

Early the next morning, I woke to a bright sun shining in a blue sky. After gulping down a quick cup of coffee, Glad and I drove directly to the gardens, anxious to see if any damage had been done. During the drive, the visible evidence of a hard frost quickly dampened my faith.

"It just isn't possible," I thought to myself. "With such an extensive frost, how could *our* gardens survive?"

Finally we drove over that last shaded stretch of road, before bursting out into the bright sunlight which was quick-thawing the steaming fields. Stopping the car on the main road, I shaded my eyes and looked out over our gardens, bracing myself for the worst. I could hardly believe what I saw.

"If that doesn't beat all!" I remarked. "There

157

doesn't seem to be a trace of frost on our garden *anywhere!* But look at the neighboring field—see the dark edges on those squash vines? They're frozen!" Only a narrow dirt lane separated the two fields, but on one side the plants were wilted and dying, while on our side—God's side—everything was all right!

Getting out of the car, I turned to appraise a small garden across the road from ours. It too bore the telltale signs of frost. Just to be sure, though, we began a quick walk-through inspection of our garden. Sure enough, our plants were green and healthy looking, with no sign of frost damage.

"I suppose I'd better confess this," I laughed. "Last night, when I suggested we pray instead of covering all this stuff, my aching back was the motivating force." I paused and looked over the fields again. "But when I see what God has done, it humbles me. One thing is certain: who can figure Him out? He works in such mysterious ways and answers the craziest prayers!"

Just as they had planned the women preserved the vegetables that fall; and when the snow was deep and the weather cold, they gave them all away. Their project proved to be a blessing to many people.

And so it went. Out of a hidebound, conservative, New England town came a move of the Spirit that marked the beginning of the charismatic renewal in that part of the country. Our fellowship rapidly grew into a true Spirit-filled community—although I must be quick to confess that we didn't have all the answers. The baptism in the Spirit is not a cure for every problem. There were times

158

when it seemed as though our prayers were not heard, and when people and conditions remained unchanged; yet we stood solidly on the Word of God. He does hear!

We also learned (the hard way) that the Master's gracious moving in our lives today doesn't exempt us from a "battle royal" next week. One principle emerged, however: we must trust Him and be totally dependent on Him for *everything*, regardless. He'll always make good His Word—although His methods can be truly mysterious.

In the midst of all this happiness, I also became aware of an inexplainable restlessness growing inside of me. I couldn't understand it: the work was growing, and people were responding to our ministry. But still the persistent thought kept returning that somewhere, beyond my home town, Jesus had something more. But where?

The answer came one Sunday morning in the spring. About an hour before Sunday school began, I drove to Saxton's River to pick up a carload of children. We were to have a guest speaker that day: Gerald Derstine, a Spirit-filled Mennonite from Pennsylvania. I passed the old Bartonsville covered bridge with its rustic, weather-beaten boards and quaint sign still tacked above its entrance:

WAGONS 5 MPH
HORSES AT A TROT

Vermont with its open country was so pleasant that I could only stop and praise the Lord. What enjoyment to feel so free! I knew the joy I felt was more than natural appreciation—so I began worshiping and praising God. Then a voice spoke to me.

"You'll soon be in Sarasota."

At first I dismissed it as *my* thoughts; but the voice spoke again, deeply impressing my mind: "You'll soon be in Sarasota."

"What does that mean, Lord? Where *is* Sarasota?"

"You'll soon be there and working for me."

I knew Glad and I had no desire to leave Vermont. Our home was there; our families were there; our church was there. Why leave when we had everything we could want or desire?

I pondered the meaning of this as I drove back to the church. Glad was talking with several people by the entrance when I arrived.

"Glad," I interrupted, taking her arm and leading her aside, "where is Sarasota?"

"In New York, near Troy, isn't it?"

"No, that's Saratoga. I've already thought of that."

"Why do you want to know?" she asked.

"The Lord—I'm sure it was the Lord—spoke to me this morning and said we'd soon be there."

Before we discussed it any further, we were interrupted by Lyle Frink. "Chuck, I think the speaker's here. The car has Pennsylvania plates."

A woman and two men came through the front door and approached me.

"I'm Gerald Derstine," the short man said, beaming an infectious smile as he thrust out his hand toward me. "This is Joe Delp and his wife, Fannie."

Gerald was the first contact our fellowship had

160

had with the charismatic movement outside Vermont. The testimony he gave us concerning the outpouring of the Spirit among the Mennonites could well be called the twenty-ninth chapter of Acts. That service had a touch of heaven on it, and several people present were filled with the Spirit.

Walking our guests to their car after the service, I noticed a bright yellow sign on Gerald's blue Chrysler:

THE GOSPEL CRUSADE, INC.
SARASOTA, FLORIDA

Stopping, I nudged Glad. "See that? Sarasota is in Florida. Suppose that has anything to do with what I heard?"

Little did I realize then that in a few days the Lord would speak to us in our living room and tell us to sell our home and let Him be our sole source. We obeyed, but not without some reluctance and many questions.

About a year later we were located in Sarasota, living in one of the Gospel Crusade's trailers and preparing to enter a ministry that would finally take us all over the world.

CHAPTER EIGHTEEN

"SQUEEZE MY HAND"

The sheer excitement of our new life in Christ has never ceased to amaze me. What a contrast to the dull, humdrum life we lived as Jehovah's Witnesses—when the most exciting thing that ever happened was a good hot argument with somebody about "the meaning of Hades"!

But we also had our heartaches. In fact, part of the excitement of this life was in watching God solve more and more complicated problems, as we placed our faith in Him.

After we'd been in Sarasota for some time, we had the opportunity of watching God work in one of the most desperate situations we had ever faced. . . .

"I wonder why Dave's late?" Glad remarked, glancing at the clock on the kitchen wall. "It's five-thirty. He should be home by now." Glad had been keeping a strict schedule since taking on a job at a local restaurant.

I watched her put the finishing touches on supper. Saturday evening was one of the few nights of the week the whole family (David, 15, Darlene, 12, Deborah, 10, and Deanna, 6—plus Glad and me) was together. David worked for the Sarasota Tribune, bundling papers. He usually got home about five.

At 5:55 the phone rang. Glad lifted the receiver from the hook and handed it to me.

"Mr. Trombley? This is Bob Hawkins. Your son's had an accident. I just delivered him to Sarasota Memorial. He's in the emergency room, and they've called in a neurosurgeon. You'd better get right down there."

Dropping the phone on the hook, I whirled toward Glad. "Dave's had a wreck! That was Hawkins' Ambulance Service. They just took him to Sarasota Memorial and called in a neurosurgeon!"

I watched the color drain from her cheerful face. The paper reported at least one serious motorcycle accident daily, many of them fatal. I had objected to Dave's buying a motorcycle, fearful that one day something like this would happen. At fifteen, however, Dave was going through a period of questioning and minor rebellion, and I had finally given in to his pleas.

Glad talked briefly with the three girls, and in a few moments we were on our way to the hospital, some fifteen minutes away.

"Listen, Glad," I said, "I don't know how badly he's hurt, but I don't suppose they would've called in a neurosurgeon unless it was serious. You pray while I drive!"

"Lord," she began, "our family belongs to You. You've never failed to guide us. When the children were small, we dedicated them to You and asked You to take them Home if You saw they were going to drift away and not serve You. If this is what

163

You're doing, we accept it and praise You for it." She continued to verbalize our simple trust in His Word.

When we arrived, I noticed a deputy sheriff asking questions outside the emergency room. Inside, several people dressed in white were grouped around an operating table. Before I got three steps into the room, someone tried to push me out.

"That's my son!" I said, and forced my way past them.

Several nurses and attendants were trying to hold Dave down. I glimpsed a white bandage wrapped around his head just above the eyes and saw the red stain oozing through it. A nurse was trying to clean his face while another removed his clothes. A young man held a suction tube to his mouth. A resident doctor had just completed a tracheotomy.

"I'm his father and would like to pray for him," I said, but was only pushed toward the door.

Glad and I slipped by an attendant and she laid her hands on Dave's head and started to pray softly. Turning, I grabbed his shoulder and tried to stop his violent thrashing. "David, this is Dad! Listen to me! It's going to be all right!"

"Mr. Trombley," a doctor said, "I'm sorry, but your son cannot hear you now. We're doing all we can for him so please leave the room!"

Pacing to and fro in the corridor, I recognized one of the attendants as he darted out of the emergency room.

"Larry! How is Dave?"

"Brother Trombley! Is that Dave in there? I didn't even recognize him. His face is really messed up." He was visibly shocked when he realized for the first time whose life he was desperately trying to

164

save. David and he had been good friends and church buddies.

"Pray while you work, will you, Larry?"

Turning, I saw the deputy sheriff. We followed him into a small room, where we could talk away from the feverish activity in the hall.

"Do you know what happened?" I asked him.

"Yes, your son was proceeding north on highway 41 just south of Bee Ridge Road, when a '50 Chevy station wagon made an improper turn directly in front of him. Your son hit on the right side where the front door connects to the fender. The force propelled him into and through the car's windshield. That's all we know at the present."

Dr. Wallace, the neurosurgeon, entered the room. Seeing me, he said, "Are you Mr. Trombley?"

"Yes, I am."

"Will you come with me, please?"

We followed him into a large consultation room. Picking up one of two X-rays from the table, he held it to the brightly-lit viewer.

"This is a picture of your son's skull. See those lines? They're fractures. See that spot there?" He pointed to a small dark place in the center of the picture. "That's a blood clot. If I don't remove that immediately, there isn't any way your son can live. But I must be honest with you; it's in a critical part of the brain. I'll do my best, but I can't guarantee anything. He may or may not make it. It's very doubtful, but I need your permission to try."

"Of course, Dr. Wallace," I replied without any hesitation. "Can you tell us anything more? What is the extent of his injuries?"

"There's severe bleeding. We've done a tracheotomy so he won't choke on his own blood. It'll
take around three and a half hours for this type of
surgery, so try to relax. I'll keep you informed, and
we'll certainly do our very best." He started to
leave.

Taking his hand in mine, I said, "You'll find us
in the chapel praying when you're through. God
bless you!"

Leaving the room, we walked slowly down the
long, lonely corridor toward the little chapel. Many
times I'd prayed with others under similar circumstances; now it was my turn.

I found it nearly impossible to pray, even in
tongues. Although I knew and trusted Jesus without reservation, my mind and feelings played tricks
on me. I tried to read the Gideon Bible but
couldn't. All I could do was feebly praise Jesus for
His past goodness to us.

Glad left in a few minutes to call the girls at
home and explain the situation to them. We also
agreed that she should call several of our prayer
partners across the nation. Seconds stretched into
minutes, and minutes seemed like eternities. I
looked at my watch. Only a few minutes had
passed.

Glad finally returned and told me she had held
back most of the details from the children until we
could tell them personally. I tried to cheer her up.
Her eyes were red and swollen.

Time dragged on. Friends filtered in and out of
the chapel. My mind began to torture me with all
kinds of negative thoughts—but I had learned long
ago that this is the time to confess His Word regardless of feelings. The more I praised Him and

166

confessed my faith in His promises, the more assurance I felt.

An hour and a half later, Dr. Wallace stuck his head around the corner. He had said the operation would take three and a half hours, but less than half that time had passed.

"Dr. Wallace! Is everything all right?" I asked as I jumped up and started toward him.

"Reverend, I've done all I can for now. That boy's brain was shredded. I had to pick pieces of hair and road dirt from his brain before I could sew it up. There's considerable swelling already, so I left the bone flap out. This will help release the pressure. If he makes it, I can do a plastic repair without any problem."

"How is he?"

"He's in Intensive Care. You can see him in a few minutes. However, there are a few things you should know. Because of the type of injury, he'll never remember anything about the accident. The laceration to the right side of his brain was so gross, he'll probably never use the left side of his body again. With therapy, he might learn to adjust. But, Reverend, he's a badly hurt boy."

Turning to Glad, who stood beside me, he studied her for a second. "I want to remind you again that I can't give you any hope for his recovery. Mrs. Trombley, I don't want you to have *any* hope. Just keep your fingers crossed. He'll be in a deep coma and may never come out of it."

"You said you removed dirt and hair from his brain. Was his skull fractured *that* badly?" I couldn't imagine what he was trying to explain.

"He has several fractures in the frontal, temporal, and parietal areas. The right side of his brain is badly macerated. I cleaned it up and repaired it the best I could. The right meningeal artery was torn, leaving part of the brain mushy. The whole area of the brain was grossly hemorrhagic from both arteries and veins. The purpose of the craniotomy was to remove the clot and control the internal bleeding."

Momentarily I stood speechless, the doctor's words meaningless.

"Thank you, doctor."

Leaving him, we hurried to the second floor and arrived at the Intensive Care Unit in time to see nurses adjusting straps across David's chest. I noticed that both his hands and feet were tied to the side of the bed. Already his face was visibly swollen and his eyes were turning a deep purple. His head was sheathed in a helmet of gauze and stretch bandages. A thin green tube connected his tracheotomy to a gurgling oxygen bottle. A nose drain was taped to his face, and intravenous tubes were in both of his arms.

My stomach was sick. Dave lay there, deathly silent, with only the hissing and bubbling of the oxygen machine and the click, click of the heart machine breaking the silence.

Glad stood on one side of the bed, I on the other. Joining our hands across his body, we prayed silently: "Lord, he's Yours, so take good care of him for us. According to Mark 11:23,24, whatever we desire in our hearts and believe that we have, we shall receive. We thank you right now for Dave's complete recovery." I squeezed Glad's warm hand. What a strength in a time like this to have a believing companion!

An R.N. quietly slipped to the bedside and told

us that we were allowed only five minutes every hour. Reluctantly, we left and sat down in the ICU waiting room outside the door.

Shortly, Dr. Wallace came by to check on Dave again. "There isn't anything you can do here, so why don't you both go home and get some rest? Your other children need you too. If there's any change, we'll call you immediately."

After he left, Glad said, "Chuck, why don't *you* go home? I'll nap here just in case Dave should wake up and call for us." I wanted to stay as badly as she did, but what the doctor said was true; somebody would have to be with the other children. When I left, Glad was curled up on the couch.

Early the next morning I returned to the hospital, to be informed by both Glad and the nurses that there had been no change in Dave, except for the tremendous swelling of his head.

"Mrs. Tombley," Dr. Wallace said when he entered ICU on his morning rounds, "I understand you stayed here last night."

"I only wanted to be near David in case he woke up."

"That's noble—but if you don't get your rest, I'll have *you* for a patient also."

Turning to me he said, "Take her home now. I'll call if I need you."

We left the hospital reluctantly. When we arrived home, Glad bravely retold the incident to the girls with as much courage and positiveness as she could muster. The three girls were visibly upset, so we took time to pray with them.

Glad tried to rest but found it impossible. Unable to rest myself, I reached for E. W. Kenyon's book, *Jesus The Healer*. I needed something that would build my faith—but my mind still refused to cooperate.

We went back to the hospital around two o'clock and asked the ICU nurse about Dave's temperature. We anticipated some difficulty here. Dr. Wallace had said the road dirt deeply imbedded in the brain might cause some infection, with a resultant rise in temperature. He said he would order massive doses of antibiotics to combat probable infection.

"His temp is up a little, but nothing to worry about," the nurse replied. "Any craniotomy reacts that way. He's resting comfortably."

Our first five-minute visit on the day following the accident was one filled with questions. Outwardly, there wasn't any change. Dave's eyes were somewhat darker and his head swollen a little more.

"How long will he be in a coma?" I asked the nurse.

"Nature has its own way of preventing him from waking. He'd have an Excedrin number 9 headache if he woke now. There really isn't any way of telling." She was kind but businesslike.

Again Glad and I stood with our hands clasped over his bed and prayed to the Lord in tongues. Looking at Dave, I found it easier to minister than before. His face was swollen beyond recognition. Momentarily, I wasn't conscious he was my son.

Late that afternoon, Dave was still in a deep coma. The nurse who maintained a constant vigil at the foot of his bed told us there had been no voluntary movement of his body. Had it not been for the heart machine, we could have assumed him dead. Both Glad and I were concerned about his lack of response.

The next morning we felt that a stronger excercise of faith was necessary—but how? Then the Lord brought to my remembrance an article I had read in *Guideposts* about an experience of Dr. William Standish Reed, a dear friend and surgeon from Tampa. It seems a young girl from Louisiana was nearly killed in an auto accident, which left her with convulsions. Her brain was so badly damaged that she should have died. When the girl's mother asked Dr. Reed to pray for her, he suggested that she treat her daughter as though she were already well, by talking with her and visiting with her. Dr. Bill's thought was: *God is Spirit; this girl is spirit; and although we can't reach her senses because of the extensive brain damage, we can commune with God and ask Him to touch her spirit.* So the mother did what Dr. Bill suggested, and eventually the girl recovered completely. His method was unorthodox, but why not try it?

When we entered ICU, I had a new sense of direction. Glad and I positioned ourselves on opposite sides of Dave's bed, after carefully pulling the curtains and closing ourselves off from prying eyes.

Taking his paralyzed left hand in mine, I leaned over and said softly but clearly in Dave's ear: "Dave, this is Dad. Can you hear my voice? If you can, then squeeze my hand!"

Slowly the seconds ticked away. Nothing happened. Then my mind began asserting itself again: "Nothing will happen. Don't make a fool of yourself!"

Again, I applied the principle of faith. I resisted the negative thoughts, blotting them out with praise to Jesus.

171

"Squeeze my hand, in Jesus' name!" I continued to wait, while Glad prayed in tongues.

"Squeeze my hand, Dave. In Jesus' name!"

More moments passed, while we continued to praise God in tongues. My hand was gently laid in Dave's, waiting for some movement.

"Dave, in Jesus' name, hear me! Squeeze my hand!"

Then gently, but very definitely, he squeezed my hand. It wasn't much, but it was sure. Before I could restrain myself, everything within me exploded.

"Hallelujah!" I shouted—and just as the nurse turned around to quiet me, Dave kicked both of his legs.

"Did you see that?" she said excitedly.

I wanted to shout, laugh, and cry all at the same time. Hours of standing on His word without any visible evidence had charged my emotions to explosive levels. From that moment, nothing would be able to stand in front of me. Like Elijah, I saw a cloud the size of a man's hand—not large to be sure, but a definite sign. Dave was still in a coma, but I had greater assurance than ever that the battle was already won.

CHAPTER NINETEEN

PLAY A G CHORD

Uneventful days passed. Dave's brain swelling receded slightly. His eyes were blacker than one could imagine. The doctor closed the tracheotomy incision in his throat, but the tube in his nose remained for feeding. As the days dragged on, it seemed he wasn't going to come out of the coma.

And then a new enemy challenged me, in the form of some of the nurses. Because my faith was strong, I'd bounce into ICU with a smile on my face, pray with Dave, and then confidently minister to others. My "unintelligent" faith bothered some of them.

"You'd better face the facts. He'll have to have speech therapy," one of them said negatively.

Another time I was warned about his language, *when* and *if* he woke up. "He'll probably use foul language; most of them do." Their purpose was to prepare me for the worst.

Once, during a visit, Glad noticed a brown paper bag taped to the head of Dave's bed. When we opened it, we found it filled with bloody hair.

"Nurse," I called. "What is this mess for?"

"We were ordered to save that. It's his hair. The undertaker asked that we save it for him—just in case."

"Get it out of here and don't let me see it again!" I snapped. They were good nurses, but they didn't realize how Satan was using them to shake my faith.

Later I rebuked one of the nurses sharply. Her continual negative talk got to me. "Would you please be still and not talk to me at all? I'm believing God's Word, and, I don't need your kind of doubt pulling me down. If you can't help me, don't talk to me at all!"

"But, Mr. Trombley, you ought to face reality," she replied. "You're a minister and you're acting immature. Your son is still in critical condition and the prognosis is guarded, so you're only making it harder on yourself." I left her and made sure I avoided her from that time on.

On the tenth day after the accident, Dave was in a semiconscious condition. His eyes rolled uncontrollably toward that horribly injured side of his brain and his face had a decided twist toward the left—yet we rejoiced. For ten days he had cheated death and proved all predictions wrong.

The next day he opened his eyes and said weakly, "Hi!" Later he asked "Where's my Dad? I want him to pray for me."

When my obstinate nurse reported for duty on the afternoon shift, I hunted her out and said, "See, I told you so!"

"I'm so glad for you," she said. Then I explained to her why I couldn't afford to look at things in the natural, and why I must stand on God's Word regardless of the circumstances.

On the thirteenth day, they helped Dave out of bed and sat him in a chair. He looked so skinny and frail. His breath was foul from the dried blood still caked in the braces on his teeth. His head hung lazily to one side.

"Hi, Dave!" I said cheerfully as I came into the room. "How're you doing?"

"Play a G chord on me," he responded, sounding like a drunk.

"What do you mean, play a G chord? Are you all right?" I'd been giving him guitar lessons before his accident and wondered if he was more confused than I had realized.

"Dave, a G chord is a musical function. Are you trying to tell me something about your guitar?"

"No, *I'm* the guitar. Play a G chord on me," he insisted. "All these nurses do is pick on me so I must be a guitar."

I glanced at the attendant and saw him grin. Sick as Dave was, his sense of humor was still intact.

Later the attendant helped him walk a few steps; but his left foot moved clumsily—more like shuffling. An elderly, white-haired lady in the bed next to Dave's smiled and rejoiced with us in his victory.

The next day, we realized we weren't out of the woods yet. Dave was alive, but it was apparent he wasn't normal. Whenever a nurse bathed him or gave him a shot, he began shouting and couldn't be stopped. Finally the staff was forced to isolate him in a glass-enclosed room at the end of the unit. Word soon "gossiped" back that they were thinking of transferring him to the fifth-floor "psycho" ward.

Early the next morning, when Glad made her regular morning phone call to check on Dave's progress, she could hear him in the background.

"He's doing fine, Mrs. Trombley," the nurse said.

"But don't I hear him shouting?" Glad asked.

"Yes, we're going to give him a sedative to quiet him down."

"Please don't do it now!" Glad pleaded. "Every time we come, he's under sedation and we can't communicate with him. It'll take us about half an hour to cross town, but we'll be there soon. Don't give him anything, please!"

She hurried into the bedroom. "Chuck, get up!" she ordered. "The Lord wants us to go to the hospital!" Ordinarily Glad isn't bossy—but that morning she sounded like a top sergeant.

We arrived at the hospital shortly after seven-thirty. Glad stayed with me for an hour, but then had to go home to awaken the girls and get them off to school. The nurse had refrained from giving Dave the sedative, as Glad had requested, and he was very noisy. When his breakfast arrived, I tried to feed him the strained baby food. After he dribbled out several spoonfuls, I gave up. Since he was still hungry, I called the nurse and she squirted his instant breakfast down the tube in his nose.

When she taped the tube back to his face, he set up his perpetual shouting. "Dad, she's trying to kill me! Ouch! Oow . . . oow . . ." No amount of reasoning could calm him.

A call from Glad came for me at the nurses' desk. "I've been called into work, so I won't be able to come back down until after three this afternoon. You'll have to stay there. How's Dave?"

"I tried to feed him, but it's useless so far. I'm going to read the Bible and pray with him; we'll see what happens then. Pray for us!"

All morning I read my New Testament to him, and after several hours I noticed a change. He had become quiet.

"Daddy, read to me," he requested.

I continued to read, meanwhile thinking to myself, "He's calling me *Daddy*. He hasn't done that for years—not since he was a little boy." (Glad had said he seemed to have regressed to his childhood, but I had been so thrilled with his progress that I hadn't noticed. Dr. Wallace had told us he was functioning with the mind of a three-year-old child at most.)

Dave interrupted my reading around noon, to say, "Daddy, I'm going to die and go to hell."

"Why do you say that, Dave? You accepted Jesus when you were a little boy; you've been Spirit-filled for some years now. You're not going to die, Dave. Jesus has healed you!"

I got up from the chair where I was sitting and sat on the edge of the bed. "Want to tell me about it?" I asked.

"Remember those times you thought I was lying and I talked my way out of it?" he began, "well, I really *had* lied. One time I told Mom I was going to Bradenton to play baseball, when I only wanted to get out of the house."

"What did you do?"

"I played ball for a little while so I could *say* I did, but then I went to the show and saw *Rosemary's Baby.*"

"Is there anything else?"

"Once I got caught speeding through a school zone by a deputy. He took out after me. I led him into the country and finally lost him by hiding in the palmettos."

"I'm glad you're leveling with me, Dave."

His left eye was half closed; his mouth twisted downward; he stared at me dully.

"Is there anything else you should tell me now?"

I realized the Spirit was working in his heart, and I didn't want to move too fast.

"I'm not getting any better," he continued. "I hurt all over, Daddy. I can't eat and I can't think straight. What makes me cry all the time? I'm dying and I'm going to hell."

He tried to grasp my hands, but his were tied to the sides of the bed.

"Son," I said quietly, "you know God's promise is that if you'll confess these things and repent, He'll forgive you. Let's pray and settle the issue right now. Leave all the guilt with Him!"

I'd witnessed this scene many times before—the deep inner workings of the Spirit bringing forth the hidden things of the heart that were secretly tucked out of sight. Dave prayed simply but sincerely, while I praised the Lord. When he finished, we rejoiced together.

"Dad," he announced suddenly, "I'm going to Elim and train for the ministry!"

For a moment I was speechless. He had informed me on several previous occasions that Christian service wasn't for him. I probed deeply into his eyes, searching for his motives—and then I saw it!

A change!

The dullness of his eyes was gone, and his face was no longer twisted.

"Dear God!" I exclaimed within myself, "he's completely delivered!" And then looking him in the eyes, I said, "What did you say, Dave? You're going to Elim and enter the ministry?"

"That's what I said, Dad!"

Now *I* was the one who felt like I was going to slip into a coma! But Dave continued: "I've been thinking while you read to me. Perhaps God permitted this accident to stop me and turn me around so I'd go His way. I should have been killed, but He's saved me for something. What do *you* think?"

"I'm inclined to agree with you, Dave. Let me get someone to check you. Be right back."

I hurried from Dave's special room into the main area of ICU just in time to see Dr. Wallace enter.

"Dr. Wallace! How much longer does Dave have to stay here?" I asked.

"Reverend, he must quiet down and stop his shouting before we can let him go."

"Will you take a look at him?" I asked, and started walking to his room while Dr. Wallace followed.

As soon as he entered the room, he was struck with the change in Dave's appearance and attitude. Taking a small flashlight from his pocket, he lifted Dave's eyelids and examined both eyes; then he felt around his neck.

"How do you feel, Dave?"

"Good *now*, Dr. Wallace. I don't hurt any more. Can I have these restraints off please?" Dave asked.

"I'll leave an order for the nurse," the surgeon replied. "But if you put your hand on your head even once, I'll put them back on and leave them there. Do you understand me? And David—*be quiet!*"

Without waiting for an answer, he turned and walked briskly to the nurse's station and wrote something on David's chart. In a moment the nurse removed the restraints from both hands and legs and put a different gown on him. As she left, Dave spoke to her.

"Nurse, what can I have to eat?"

Startled, she turned back toward him. "Would you like some ice cream or something to drink?"

"Both!"

When the orderly set a chocolate milk shake on the stand beside his bed, Dave reached for it with his left hand. It was steady and strong. Taking the spoon, he fed himself, swallowing without any difficulty. God had completely healed him, and I was so filled with gratitude and praise that I could hardly keep from shouting.

Between mouthfuls he said, "Know what? I've never had a testimony before, but I've got one now."

"You sure have, Dave," I said. "You sure have."

The following Sunday morning, when Dave was released from the hospital, it was bright and sunny. His steps were slow and labored, but sure. After thanking the nurses for their care, we made our way to the entrance where I had the car parked. I watched as he seated himself carefully in the front seat, guarding his head. He was missing about eight square inches of skull which would have to be replaced. Until then, he would have to be especially careful to avoid injury.

"Dave, it's been more than three weeks since you were home. Where to? Home or church?

"It's Sunday, isn't it? Church!"

"Hallelujah, David! Hallelujah!"

Comments and inquiries, or requests for speaking engagements, books or cassette teaching-tapes should be directed to:

Charles C. Trombley, Director
Charismatic Teaching Ministries, Inc.
Post Office Box 15308
Tulsa, Oklahoma 74115

BIBLIOGRAPHY

Charles Trombley was a Jehovah's Witness before being converted to biblical Christianity—a miracle which came about through the miraculous healing of his daughter's clubfeet. As wonderful as that was, only a Jehovah's Witness can understand the problems it created!

After his conversion, Trombley went through valleys of heartache and rejection, and through tunnels of personal doubts and questions. But finally, after a long search, he entered into a deeper spiritual experience which completely liberated him from cultism.

Since his deeper experience in the Spirit, he has furthered his education at Immanuel Baptist College and has had a wide ministry as a dynamic teacher. He is the editor of The Expositor Publications, a company which specializes in helpful Christian literature for Jehovah's Witnesses, and he has authored several books.

Mr. Trombley's interesting background makes him uniquely qualified to discern truth from error, and to explain the significance of the great charismatic awakening that is having such an impact on the Church today. He has served on the faculty of Trinity Bible College, as well as being the secretary of Gospel Crusade, Inc. Recently he resigned his preaching position in one of the largest Full Gospel churches in the Southwest to found and direct Charismatic Teaching Ministries, Inc., an organization devoted to ministering to the whole Body of Christ nationally. Trombley is in great demand as a conference speaker, and has spoken to more than two hundred Full Gospel Business Men's chapter meetings. He has also spoken at colleges, and only recently addressed the ambassadors and representatives at the United Nations.

WHEREVER PAPERBACKS ARE SOLD
OR USE THIS COUPON

Whitaker House

504 LAUREL DRIVE
MONROEVILLE, PA 15146

SEND INSPIRATIONAL BOOKS
LISTED BELOW

Title	Price	☐ Send Complete Catalog
_____	_____	
_____	_____	
_____	_____	
_____	_____	
_____	_____	
_____	_____	
_____	_____	
_____	_____	

Name _____

Street _____

City _____ State _____ Zip _____

Suggested Inspirational Paperback Books

FACE UP WITH A MIRACLE
by Don Basham $1.25

>   This is a fascinating book about God the Holy
>   Spirit bringing a new dimension into the lives
>   of twentieth-century Christians. It is filled
>   with experiences that testify to a God of mir-
>   acles being unleashed in our lives right now.

BAPTISM IN THE HOLY SPIRIT: COMMAND OR
OPTION?   by Bob Campbell $1.25

>   A teaching summary on the Holy Spirit, cover-
>   ing the three kinds of baptisms, the various
>   workings of the Holy Spirit, the question of
>   tongues and how to know when you have re-
>   ceived the Baptism of the Spirit.

A SCRIPTURAL OUTLINE OF THE BAPTISM
IN THE HOLY SPIRIT   by George and
Harriet Gillies   60¢

>   Here is a very brief and simple outline of the
>   Baptism in the Holy Spirit, with numerous
>   references under each point. This handy little
>   booklet is a good reference for any question
>   you might have concerning this subject.

A HANDBOOK ON HOLY SPIRIT BAPTISM
by Don Basham $1.25

>   Questions and answers on the Baptism in the
>   Holy Spirit and speaking in tongues. The book
>   is in great demand, and answers many impor-
>   tant questions from within the contemporary
>   Christian church.

HE SPOKE, AND I WAS STRENGTHENED
by Dick Mills $1.25

>   An easy-to-read devotional of 52 prophetic
>   scripturally-based messages directed to the
>   businessman, the perfectionist, the bereaved,
>   the lonely, the ambitious and many more.

SEVEN TIMES AROUND
by Bob and Ruth McKee
$1.25

A Christian growth story of a family who receives the Baptism in the Holy Spirit and then applies this new experience to solve the family's distressing, but frequently humorous problems.

LET GO!
by Fenelon
95¢

Jesus promised a life full of joy and peace. Why then are so many Christians struggling to attain the qualities that Christ said belonged to the child of God? Fenelon speaks firmly—but lovingly to those whose lives have been an up hill battle. Don't miss this one.

VISIONS BEYOND THE VEIL
by H. A. Baker
95¢

Beggar children who heard the Gospel at a rescue mission in China, received a powerful visitation of the Holy Spirit, during which they saw visions of Heaven and Christ which cannot be explained away. A new revised edition.

DEAR DAD, THIS IS TO ANNOUNCE MY DEATH
by Ric Kast
$1.25

The story of how rock music, drugs and alcohol lead a youth to commit suicide. While Ric waits out the last moments of life, Jesus Christ rescues him from death and gives him a new life.

GATEWAY TO POWER
by Wesley Smith
$1.25

From the boredom of day after day routine and lonely nights of meaningless activity, Wes Smith was caught up into a life of miracles. Dramatic healings, remarkable financial assistance, and exciting escapes from dangerous situations have become part of his life.

SIGI AND I
by Gwen Schmidt

95¢

The intriguing narration of how two women smuggled Bibles and supplies to Christians behind the Iron Curtain. An impressive account of their simple faith in following the Holy Spirit.

MINISTERING THE BAPTISM
IN THE HOLY SPIRIT   by Don Basham

$1.00

Over 100 received their Baptism after hearing the author give this important message. The book deals with such topics as the Baptism as a second experience, the primary evidence of the Baptism, and tongues and the "Chronic Seeker."

THE LAST CHAPTER
by A. W. Rasmussen

$1.25

An absorbing narrative based on the author's own experience, in the charismatic renewal around the world. He presents many fresh insights on fasting, church discipline and Christ's Second Coming.

A HANDBOOK ON TONGUES, INTERPRETATION
AND PROPHECY   by Don Basham

$1.25

The second of Don Basham's Handbook series. Again set up in the convenient question and answer format, the book addresses itself to further questions on the Holy Spirit, especially the vocal gifts.